LIFE LESSONS FROM SPIRITUALITY AND NATURE

GHAZALA ANJUM

INDIA · SINGAPORE · MALAYSIA

ISBN

Paperback: 979-8-89699-798-6

Hardcase: 979-8-89906-985-7

Dedicated to my beloved mother,

the late Mrs. Siraj Fathima

DISCLAIMER

This book is nonfiction. As the author, I have made every effort to recount the anecdotes and experiences that shaped my journey accurately. The content is based on my personal recollections, which may contain minor imperfections or lapses in detail. Any similarities to the experiences of others are purely coincidental.

Neither the author nor the publisher provides personal, professional, or spiritual advice through this book.

While every effort has been made to ensure the book is free of errors, inadvertent grammatical or typographical mistakes may remain. The author and the publisher accept no responsibility for any loss or damage and are not liable for any issues resulting from such errors.

– Ghazala Anjum

CONTENTS

ACKNOWLEDGMENTS

'Every little moment of pain and smile counts as an investment in reflecting the essence.'

At the outset, I express my deepest gratitude and reverence to my beloved parents, the Late Mrs. Siraj Fathima and Mr. Fareeduddin Ansari, for their dua and blessings.

I am deeply grateful to my dear husband, Dr. Justice Shameem Akther, for his cooperation and encouragement in all my endeavors. I also appreciate the affection and support of my siblings and everyone else. I greatly cherish the love and contributions of my dear children, Husna, Zeeshan, and their families.

I genuinely appreciate Dr. Nirmala Rita Nair's exceptional kindness and encouraging support. I am truly grateful to Dr. Sridhar and Aarthi Vaddeboina for their motivation and significant contributions, which have profoundly impacted this work. I also thank Sunitha Sarwaday for her valuable suggestions and careful review of Hindi verses. I appreciate my niece Almas for her quick help with the final revisions of the Hindi verses. I also thank all my dear friends for their continued inspiration. I sincerely thank Notion Press and the publishing team for their support and guidance.

A simple note of gratitude can lead to significant outcomes, as reflected in my experience, which has opened the door for this work.

FOREWORD

"Life Lessons from Spirituality and Nature" by Ms. Ghazala Anjum, former Assistant Professor, is an unusual blend of memoir and bilingual poetry. It allows for ornate flourishes of language and a restrained English version, making it an enjoyable and unforgettable experience. The writer skillfully weaves together recollections of the past, fascination with the 'mesmerizing' bounties of nature in her garden, and her journey of self-discovery with a celebration of life. We recognize the positive emotions of love, joy, serenity, and awe as we read it. It calls to mind what the German poet Heinrich von Kleist wrote: "Happiness cannot be proven like a mathematical theorem. It must be felt if it is to exist."

The work exudes peace and quiet joy. The writer expresses her deepest thoughts and shares glimpses of her past. She also reveals various positive practices, such as using her morning and evening walks to admire nature, listen to music, and listen to spiritual discourses. She uses this time to count her blessings and practice gratitude daily.

Ms. Anjum has not only painted word pictures of her garden with its flowers but also gives us a feel of the peaceful atmosphere. She appreciates the sights and sounds of nature in the quiet hours of dusk, dawn, and quiet starlit nights. The work evokes in the reader an appreciation of beauty, of the quiet times that make it possible to sit in tranquility, introspect, and think about things that need to be sorted out.

What stands out is the writer's heightened awareness of the sights and sounds of nature and her ability to see beauty in the everyday world around us. She marvels at the extraordinary beauty of the star-studded skies. She considers "munificent" nature, "the best creation of God," to be enchanting and a remedy for many ills. The impact of nature on her life is evident in that the soothing, refreshing effect of her walks in the calm, peaceful atmosphere enables her to make some of her life's best decisions.

'Bittersweet memories' and joyous moments remind her of family and friends. She believes Life is all about what we treasure and value, and emotions are essential to our lives. Her ability to convey her thoughts with brevity is evident when she describes the city of Hyderabad.

Her gift of descriptive writing and ability to paint vivid pictures gives us glimpses of her reflections and feelings of contentment. Her language is embellished with figurative speech. To her, 'life is a journey,' and the journey in the sky parallels her life's journey.

Memories are a recurrent theme, and some of these memories are disturbing, but she uses the weapon of a calm mind to challenge these thoughts. This conscious effort to calm herself and think things through is just one example of her emotional intelligence, her ability to recognize and manage her emotions. As she states, "Consciousness is the key to success."

Her introspective nature enhances her *self-awareness*, aids in making decisions, and helps her lead a more fulfilling life. She is grateful that she turned to spirituality, which she feels is the best thing that has happened to her. She reflects on her journey, what is meaningful in life, and aspects that are significant beyond our everyday lives. She finds "consolation, understanding, assurance, solutions, forgiveness, and much more."

As she looks back, she realizes that experiences have taught her to be strong during difficult, demanding times and find solutions in peace. The secret of her serene life lies in her ability to replace disturbances with calm and quiet, which bring 'wisdom, humility, discipline and a clear conscience.'

Her quest for inner peace leads to introspection and heart-searching, and her habits of reframing her thoughts, mastering her emotions, and practicing gratitude enable her to achieve the best version of herself.

This conscious effort to attain inner peace, which no one can give us but ourselves, is therapeutic and restorative and reminds us of the words of Eckhart Tolle," You find peace not by rearranging the circumstances of your life, but by realizing who you are at the deepest level." The writer did not merely wish for peace. She thought, acted, and lived in a way that showed compassion, calmness, equanimity, a better understanding of herself and others, enriched her world, and radiated peace and positivity to those around her.

– Dr. Nirmala Rita Nair

Former Professor & Head

Dept. of English

Muffakham Jah College of Engg. & Tech.

Hyderabad

PROLOGUE

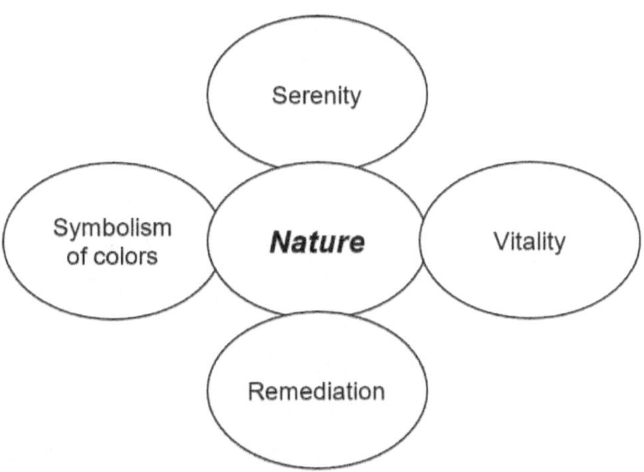

It was one of those beautiful January misty winter mornings in Hyderabad; embracing nature's verdure and serenity, I started my morning walk around the Government-provided Bungalow with my headphones on, listening to music and some engaging lectures while appreciating the mesmerizing bounties of nature. It took me into deep thoughts, with an insight into the voyage to reality. Amidst the beautiful flora and fauna, my mind stays active, and my heart pumps great energy, adding to my well-being. During these walks, my mind replayed so many fascinating life stories, and one of those noteworthy fascinations of my childhood was the majestic district collector's bungalow guarded by security near my home. As a curious young kid filled with enthusiasm, I used to sneak inside through the gate.

After twenty-five years, destiny drove me into a similar bungalow when my husband joined the judicial service. After a few job transfers, we landed in Hyderabad and spent several years in a similar bungalow. I kept on counting the blessings, especially during these walks. The 19th day of 2023 was the last day spent in that dream bungalow; the frondescent greenery, very much in the lap of Mother Nature, away from city pollution, made it notably special.

Every morning, waking up to the melody of chirping birds was a real treat to my ears. Morning walks were a quotidian thing every day; the enchanting variety of colorful flowers in the garden, the smell of the mud, the sight of wasps and bees collecting nectar from the cascade of pretty flowers, and the grandeur and the peacefulness of nature made the environment so surreal. In awe of watching the flock of pigeons identifying you and waiting to land for grains was a regular thing. That was an incredible encounter each day that could entertain any soul. For me, the favored routine was watching the pigeons resting on the lawns, quenching their thirst, and soaking themselves in small clay cups filled with water to the brim. Each step during these walks reminded me of the countless blessings bestowed upon me.

"In every walk with nature, one receives far more than he seeks."
John Muir

I enjoyed the soothing musical notes with a hot cup of tea on the pleasant evenings in my backyards. The serenity of the clear sky during the calm nights, with countless shining stars, added to the incredible moments of picturesque beauty full of aesthetic appeal; it reminded me of my childhood days attempting to count the stars, losing count, and starting over, immersed in the enthusiasm of childhood innocence. All these sights and memories of earthly paradise often took me to an unheard-of world, away from chaos. Indubitably, nature is the best creation of God, which nurtures you immensely and offers priceless refreshments beyond imagination.

It is when I discovered that bountiful, munificent nature is a great blessing that enthralls you and remedies many ills. The calmness and serenity during these walks enabled me to make some of my life's best decisions of that time. With profound pleasure, I admit that all this calmness had a tranquilizing effect on my mind and made me lively by harnessing its power. Undoubtedly, a piece of my heart will miss the whole thing in perpetuity.

ज़िंदगी की खट्टी मीठी यादों में खोया है ये दिल

यादें तो बहुत हैं कुछ रूह को टटोले, तो कई छूले दिल

घर, परिवार, दोस्त, रिश्ते नाते, सब हैं रंग बिरंगे मोती अनमोल

ये मोती जो सजाए बगीचे, बनकर ज़ेवर, लता बेल और रंग बिरंगे फूल

Bittersweet memories of life make the heart and mind flutter and wonder,

The soul-touching chords of happiness awaken the heart to fond Memories!

Kinfolk and friends, the connecting fibers, the colorful precious pearls, beautifully entwined

As radiant, multicolored blooms, climbers, and creepers, the jewels that ornate a garden!

Life is all about what we cherish and what makes us nostalgic; everything connects to our senses and emotions. Our elders trained us to contain our emotions of happiness, resentment, sadness, etc. However, it is a fact that when someone becomes emotional during conversations and while making speeches or in reality shows, it touches our hearts and demonstrates that when something comes from the heart, it has a profound impact. Emotions are essential to our lives; as I contemplated my voice from the past, many unforgettable memories replayed in my mind! Without a shadow of a doubt, I am convinced that emotions are not heavenly but purely human.

A plethora of emotions ran through my mind on that beautiful Tuesday morning, the last day of the first month of the calendar year 2023, full of hope, freshness, and enthusiasm. I was all set to embark on a journey to the USA, I started from my home to the airport in Hyderabad.

As I was heading to the airport, seated next to the window in the car, I was amazed at the fast pace at which the City of Hyderabad had outgrown exponentially over a decade. City life of Hyderabad has its circles and cycles; the hustle and bustle of the city reminded me of the prayer then made by Mohammed Quli Qutub Shah, the founder of Hyderabad; it is said that he prayed to the Almighty to 'fill the city with people the way the river is filled with variety of fish[1].' Hyderabad has been a home to people from different parts of the nation who come down to make a living. It has turned into a huge metropolitan city with facilities provided to people, such as advanced structural aspects with numerous high-rise buildings, a little freedom from traffic hassles due to the enormous flyovers that emerged to ease the traffic chaos in the recent past, road widening, and its quality to harbor luxury cars and to accommodate foreign delegates and visitors to the city. At this moment, in a fraction of a second, numerous thoughts flashed through my mind, and my heart was en route, reminiscing.

As we reached the airport, we were rushing into a different world. Within no time, we boarded the flight from Hyderabad to

---

1 Ramanachary, K. V. Hyderabad, A Poem Come True. The Times of India, October 3, 2001. https://timesofindia.indiatimes.com/hyderabad-a-poem-come -true/articleshow/1015988637.cms.

Dubai; on the flight, I came across the enthusiastic passengers about their destinations, each face beaming with a smile, some excited first-time travelers, some frequent, some composed faces, and many more mixed expressions. The most unique thing that caught my eye was the young mothers caring for and trying to calm the toddlers and infants. It took me into a reflective mood, only to realize that some wistful, nostalgic moments touched the magical chords in the depths of my restive heart! Throughout the journey, the excitement kept me awake; I was longing to meet my children, my newlywed dear son and daughter-in-law, who were at dawn to a beautiful start of their life journey together, and my beloved daughter, son-in-law, and two grandkids, it was strange feeling much more than eagerness for my second newborn grandchild. I was impatiently waiting to take him in my arms and cuddle him, coupled with the thrilled longing for sweet, gentle hugs from my older three-year-old grandchild. Too soon, with these thoughts, my happiness knew no bounds.

औलाद का हो अपना मुकाम दुलार भरा माँ बाप के दिल में

पर नातिन होते हैं नन्हे फ़रिश्ते टुकड़े जिगर के आँख के तारे,

भोली सी मुस्कान और चुलबुली शरारतों की एक झलक के लिए तरसे ये नैन,

सामने देखा या यादों में ढूंढा इन्हे, दोनों ही सूरत में हैं भर आए ये नैन

नमी न थमे ख़ुशी में बस अपना अंदाज़ लिए झलकते हैं आंसू सनम, कम्बख्त बिना कहे,

कहें हम ख़ुद से मुस्कुरा कर इज़हारे ख़ुशी है आँखों की, इन पर हमारा इख़्तियार कहाँ!

Children enjoy unconditional love in the hearts of parents,

And grandchildren are a cut above, little angels, aortic fragments,

Moist eyes yearn for a glimpse; tears roll down on both occasions,

Whether you are far away or right in front of them, happiness is not contained!

Smiling and dabbing, eyes communicate a natural expression of joy,

oh tears! No control over them, dear!

As the flight was covering the horizons of the sky, I was ceaselessly watching the vast sky and the dark clouds playing hide and seek. It took me away from the ground level to the unimaginative soaring heights and then into nostalgic moments of my life, paralleling the journey in the sky with my life's journey. The journey significantly covers thousands of miles from one world to another, reminding us of the country's specialty. India is a land of traditions and culture, whereas the USA remains the land of dreams and opportunities. I love to travel, explore new places, and learn about diverse cultures, but my excitement gets shackled due to severe travel sickness that I sometimes suffer. In a pursuit to combat my travel sickness, with some unknown fear, I gradually slipped into my profound thoughts; my mind started hovering over and over regarding the beautiful blessings of my life.

Moreover, it is the most delightful gift of reflections, which came as products of many circles, waves, contentment, and gratitude—that moment filled me with a deep-rooted curiosity about self-discovery. Little did I know then that these deep thoughts and impressions would bring me closer to some of the most cherishing moments of my life!

Throughout the journey, a multitude of thoughts started dwelling in my mind, especially when you leave your motherland; even for a short period, you tend to miss every bit of it. On one side is the excitement of the journey and meeting my immediate family and others; on the other, concern about what you are leaving behind pops up in your mind. The vicious cycle of thinking never ceases; thoughts related to good or bad decisions taken in life, moments of significance, family affairs, blind spots, and health-related issues not only nest in your mind but start replaying. Understanding, acknowledging, and going by the flow takes a while. It happens at least till the moment you settle down.

While spending the initial few hours on the flight, some beautiful memories, specific interests, and some instances flashed through my mind. I wondered how one is influenced in many ways by numerous people, personal experiences, and circumstances around one. Growing up in a middle-class family near Hyderabad, many things fascinated me.

Each passing day connects to some emotional experiences; we all go through complex and challenging times with moments of smiles and heartaches, and the human mind longs for escape from pain. All we need to understand is that life is a journey filled with enriching experiences; despite this fast-paced evolution of technology and advancements, we often need help in the whirlwind of emotions. However, we seldom get the chance to open up and discuss; it sometimes creates a void, it is when we humans prefer intra-personal communication. I miss tossing ideas around with someone about a few things; the sharing refreshes and gives you a new perspective. More significantly, on a personal front, some instances and experiences leave a lasting impression on us. Moreover, conscientiousness is the key to success; the sooner we learn, the better it is.

The favors of God are full of surprises with amazing revelations; one needs to have a better perception to rejoice in them. I have realized that life has countless blessings, like infinite bright stars in the sky, but when we are eclipsed amidst unforeseen challenges, confronting them becomes painful, and hopelessness emerges. It is the human psyche to panic during moments of unrest; we tend to pour out our woes to others, sometimes resulting in insecurities and more turmoil, leading to risky behaviors. Consequently, the measures of our influences in life are mere soft spots and satisfaction. We meet many people; some remain with us throughout life's journey, and some leave an enduring impact on us. Eventually, the most important thing is the lessons we have learned through these encounters. Working on the intrinsic details to set things right, we must unfold treasures by exploring new ways and means without prejudices.

हर उस नीयत पर अज़मत जहाँ शराफत और सादगी हो पहचान

खुदरत के करिश्मे बेशुमार, खूब मिले सबक हर मोड़ पर!

हाँ ऐसे तो बहोत हैं आज़माइशें पर दिल को इबादत में लगाना

दुनियावि जज़्बा ए मुहोब्बत तो बहोत हैं देखे, इसे खुदा के लिए मेहफूज़ रखना,

मोहल्लत नहीं देती ज़िन्दगी, मुख्तसर है यहाँ;

और यह बाज़ार भी तो नहीं खरीदो फरोक्त या अदल बदल हो जहाँ!

Be righteous, upright, and prepared for a bitter sip; nature's miraculous magic is boundless!

Graciousness as a hallmark! Let integrity and simplicity symbolize your identity!

Passion and love are for the Maker; reserve them; devotion is worship!

Life gives no intermission or notice; it is no trade fair to merchandise!

Unfortunately, a part of society is engulfed in pride and ego, which restricts people's tolerance. In contrast, tolerance is an essential element that heals and promotes the surrender of self-conceit. So, one should eventually develop the aptitude to stretch and replace cacophonic disturbances with symphonic whispers of calmness with a touch of wisdom, humility, discipline, and a clear conscience. Hence, sooner or later, working towards attaining self-peace is a piece of therapy that helps you avoid residues of chaos, resulting in finding tranquility within the self and the spheres around you.

Within the cycles of life, I found spirituality to be the best thing that has happened to me; it has consolation, understanding, assurance, solutions, forgiveness, and much more. Everyone contrives a plan regarding coping mechanisms to deal with unforeseen challenges. My life experiences taught me to be strong during demanding times and find solutions in the pages of spiritual peace and tranquility. Further, a quest for inner peace takes you to a serene world of introspection, leading to heart-searching.

AMMI AUR ABBU

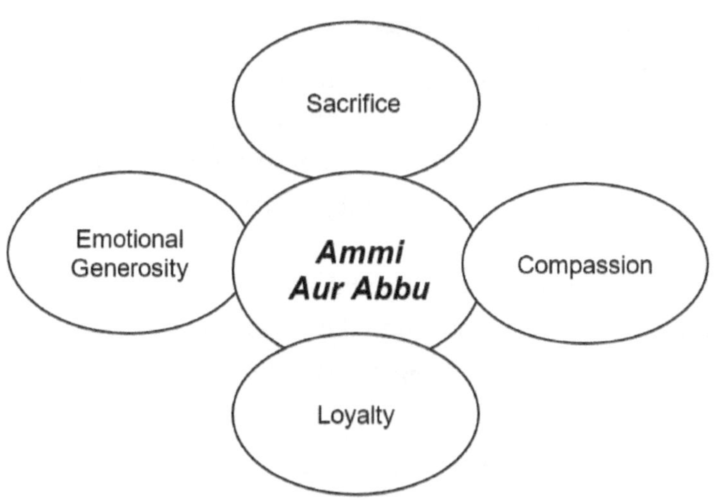

1.1 MY ROOTS-LESSONS FROM AMMI AND ABBU

Love, care, and affection are essential to safeguard inner peace and relationships among parents, children, and the entire family. They also promote harmony with the entities around us, profoundly influencing us to seek placidness. Undeniably, spiritual richness, adoration for loved ones, and close acquaintance with lush and verdant elements of nature add charm and tranquility to life. With eyes closed, a few moments of soothing talk with oneself has a calming effect on the mind and soul; it engages oneself in vivid memories that tranquilize the inner self, paving the way for an uninterrupted, quiet mind. This short period rewinds the best moments spent with all the nearest and dearest, connecting you to the euphoric moments of the past.

"In every conceivable manner, the family is a link to our past, a bridge to our future." Alex Haley

Heading off with a sappy start from home to the airport ended with our boarding the flight, and the thoughts on the expedition landed at the engaging sight of the young parents, mothers, and kids struggling to settle down on the flight. The flight attendants made the young kids feel special by capturing pictures of some selective kids, which was awe-inspiring and one-of-a-kind. Looking at the kids, I had mixed emotions, with the excitement of a family reunion in the United States after a gap of a year and a half.

Soon, it was meal serving time on the flight, and then, while the rest of the passengers were getting ready for a nap, the crew dimmed off the lights. Consequently, my thoughts slipped into the memories of my childhood travels on buses, cars, and trains. I experienced spells of whispered yearnings playing hide-and-seek in deep memory of my days spent with Ammi and Abbu.

ज़िंदगी का हर सफ़र सुहाना, सुहाने पल, सुहाने नज़ारे दूर गगन की ऊंचाइयों में!

बादलों की छुपा छुपी, ख़ूबसूरती चारों ओर मानो एक दिलकश सी तस्वीर बनाए,

दिल में समाए कई यादें लौट आए हर पल पुराने, खट्टी मीठी यादों के तराने

कभी चलते पैदल तो कभी कोई और ज़रिये से भरते उड़ान, हुए गुम इस यादों के सफ़र में

Far away in the sky! Mesmerizing moments and views,

Marvelous reminders of this life's journey, hidden in the silence of the clouds

Aesthetic appeal all around painted, memories in the heart immortal,

captured into a beautiful picture in the mind's eye! flashing back episodically

Tunes of melody and morose, Odyssey memorable,

Curiosity by numerous means soaring higher and higher!

Born in a middle-class family, my father and mother were distant relatives, and they entered into wedlock in a town in the late 1960s. They shared lovely personal bonds; their unique identities were the hallmarks that drew people closer. My father is an educated, ambitious person, a caring husband, a doting father, a committed professional, and a motivating educator. He spared no effort to provide the best for the family. In this pursuit, he sacrificed a lot and missed some vital moments of life, which he acknowledged in the later stages poignantly. However, this remains symbolic of his affinity with everyone. His service-mindedness and steadfastness as a lecturer in a government degree college and participation in other social initiatives earned him good rapport with friends, colleagues, extended families, and neighbors.

मन मोह लेने वाली यादें, निकाह जोड़े बंधन अनोखे

नींव जो प्यार से हर रिश्ता नाता जोड़े

बेहद खूबसूरत रिश्ता ऐसा

अलग हो पहचान और गुण अनेक दिल को लुभाने वाले

Unique devotion, and bonding by the wedding strong, memories heartfelt!

New closeness in cementing every bond thick and tight

Love and sacrifice wondrous, extraordinary winsome image decorated,

unique identity, and many such charming qualities paired!

I saw my mother advocating smooth relationships with everyone. She was an embodiment of kindness, gratitude, and righteousness. As a kid, I drew rich lessons from her affection and broadmindedness. She was a treasure of blessings with a beautiful innocent spark in her eyes, reflections of colors of nature in her smiles, wisdom in her sayings, and a classic approach to everything. She perfectly blended tradition, convention, and modern thoughts regarding living life and raising her eight kids. Whenever I see a bond between young parents and small kids, I watch this unique connection with boundless enthusiasm; my blossoming childhood imprints flashback. These nostalgic moments are worth re-living as they drive you with great strength.

"The joys of parents are secret, and so are their grieves and fears: they cannot utter the one, nor will they utter the other." – Francis Bacon

1.2 MY MOTHER & HER INSPIRATIONAL LESSONS

Let me unveil a few of the most inspiring stories about relationships in life: a mother is the firm foundation of a family, and a father is the architect. Siblings are the whole and sole connecting thread that keeps you intertwined throughout your life, with all the best days of togetherness spent during childhood; those memories make life distinctly unique. It is just an adynaton; such stories keep the earth spinning; however, survival through pleasant and unpleasant moments builds up an individual.

A person is not the product of family alone; the extended family, school that one attended, friends, teachers, and society we grew up with have a vital role in shaping any person! Life is not always easy; one navigates through many challenges and overcomes severe grief storms. Of course, the quality and quantity of turmoil one faces may differ; my childhood was no different, yet it remains the best phase of my life.

ममता के आँचल के हसरतों भरे फल फूल

सींचे और उभारे तुम्हे शानदार दो माली के मीत और प्रीत

न्योछावर किये सारी दुनिया हम ही पर तुलना नहीं जिसकी, बेहद अनमोल,

ख़ुशगवार था आलम, आसरे तो बहुत हैं, आपसा कौन सहारा

In the warmth of mother's lap, the fruits and blossoming flowers of childhood innocence,

Raised with the unconditional love of two excellent gardeners,

Unmatched and boundless love surrounds us like armor—Mom and Dad's affection filled our world with sparks of joy!

Many well-wishers though! who can surpass you in love, selflessness and endless sacrifice?

Hailing from a middle-class background, how I grew up in a small town with meager medical, educational, and drinking water facilities left a lot of unforgettable impressions on my mind. Back then, in the 1970s and '80s, the society and mindset of people were entirely diverse, but I consider myself fortunate to have grown up in the best setup with progressive-minded parents. The zero imposter syndrome and non-judgmental inclusiveness among people in those days make my childhood memorable.

My parents and family members were no strangers to challenges, and I had insecurities of unrest and some testing times in understanding some family ties and situations. Growing up in a large family surrounded by immediate and extended family members as a boon helped me master many real-life situations. As the epitome of the best throughout, my parents gave me the finest lessons to be grateful for the best and the worst in life, significantly contributing to making me into what I am today! Through my father's shared life experiences, the significance of being disciplined, helpful, punctual and steadfast became robust. I drew lessons in all spheres regarding what to do and what to leave behind. As the most unexcelled days, these childhood moments gave me courage, tolerance, and perseverance. With tears welled eyes and unfading smiles, I cherish the days spent with my late dear Ammi.

तुम्हीं से मिली सीख, सबक कई बेपनाह सख़ावत और दरिया दिली वाले

तुम बिन दिल बसेरा ग़ाम, तकलीफ जुदाई वाला, हर दिलचस्प चीज़ लगे फीकी,

बसा खुद में बेहिसाब डर अनजाना सा, पर सजाए हुए मुस्कान लबों पर हलकी

छुपाए दिल की तकलीफ बेशुमार समझदारी और सब्र से, तुम्हीं से है माँ सीखा अंजाने में

Every exciting thing seems dull when fear and anxiety prevail,

Caning the pain in the heart by donning an unfading generous smile,

Zillion lessons of wisdom and patience were learned from you unwittingly, Mom!

An everlasting twinkle conceals plight and makes me stand tall!

Nevertheless, not all memories bring shiny smiles; some wreak havoc. One such incident severely shook my family in 1978. I was in primary school, and we were four siblings then; that was when, as a young kid, I witnessed the first riots in the town; there was a lot of vandalism, troublemakers damaged some of our property and home, our car in the backyard was doused with gasoline and burnt to ashes, the flames of which were visible from a distance of half a kilometer, it was the scariest scene for anyone who would look at from a distance mistaken for the house to be ablaze. So was my father, completely devastated at the sight. In addition, the crockery in the kitchen rubble into bits and pieces, and the transistors and leather cases, which were part of our commercial business material stored in the drawing room, were badly sabotaged.

As a family, we could escape from the worst commotion that could happen to us. It was the first time we knew a rampage existed, significantly impacting everyone.

This mayhem left an indelible impression on the entire family. My mother, with all four children at home at that point of turmoil, managed the situation so well with her prudence by turning off the lights in the house, maintaining absolute silence, and staying composed to portray it as if there were no inmates. It left her shaken, and over time, she developed a sickness.

The reason for the uproar and the damage caused to a few in society during those days is still beyond my grasp; I have no idea where these tumults in society grew and were reflected sporadically. Fear built up among children and adults, and unrest grew daily, resulting in intense insecurities. We all were very panic-stricken, particularly at night, with threats to our lives and properties. However, blunt you might face, emotions run through you as a human. I noticed very closely how tough times of violence, destruction, and emotional oppression intimidate people, with terror shattering self-esteem and confidence. As a family, we went through frozen traumatic experiences, which left us shaken for an extended period. The menace had a long-lasting distressing impact on emotional strength and well-being of our family   as well as other victims, resulting in nightmares, psychological trauma and deep silence within. However, standing together, sharing wretched lows with our kin, and seeking their cooperation during crisis times helped us to overcome the pain powerfully. There was togetherness with no feelings of hatred among the friend circles in the neighborhood. Unity and solidarity of the kin is the best stress management technique, providing the required support system to a disturbed soul; it boosts our confidence and fills us with untold strength and energy.

People in our vicinity were amicable and harmonious at their best. We always believed in oneness, respected every culture, enjoyed an exchange of greetings on various festive occasions, exchanged unique festival special dishes, and revered one another's cultural preferences and traditions as one. All the enjoyable, cherishing moments of life during those times are still fresh in my memories. Today, when I think of particular instances, my indebtedness to our neighbors grows multifold for their benignity and support; they were always accommodating with their timely support through our thick and thin. I salute my neighbors for their kindness and generous support.

दंगे फसाद से क्या हो हासिल, डरावनी तंगदस्ती निचोड़ने वाली रूह को, हो नन्हें दिल गूँगे और बिखेरे तार दिल के

क्या बस शोहरत, जायदाद, इबादत के तरीखे नाम, रूप से है बंटता इंसान?

क्या इंसानियत का वजूद है इतना तंगदस्त? के दूरियाँ ले आए दहशत के फरमान!

कमी नहीं दरिया दिल नेकी करने वालों की इन दहशतगर्द हालात में,

भला हो, सज्जन तुम जिए हज़ारों साल! ये दुआ है मेरी मन में!

Under the guise of name, piety, patrimony, why separation, and unrest?

Divisions shatter the young hearts and shake the minds and souls!

Alas, these distances lead to the dumbness of tiny hearts!

Horror and turmoil weaken the strings of joy,

Who is to be blamed? But there still exist some doers of good!

My prayer for the gentle ones, Oh, Angels, you may live for long years!

Life in a small town during the 1970s and '80s was challenging, particularly for fetching drinking water from distant municipal water taps situated at some selective spots or water tankers delivered to colonies at regular appointed hours.

I remember my childhood struggles of carrying empty pots to fetch water, thanks to the kind tanker driver uncle, who was considerate enough to help us by opening the main tap. Life provides numerous opportunities to enlighten and bring us closer to life's struggles and lessons. This incident emphasized the importance of conserving water and helping those in need.

With time, our family grew and welcomed more kids; we became four to eight siblings, making it a family unit of ten members. However, my father was the sole breadwinner; shouldering all responsibilities might have been challenging. My father had wiser investments and a vision to provide the family with the best and cater to the large family's needs, with a decent number of visitors often. At any point, provisional sustenance was never an issue; we always had it in abundance.

Some bitter, sour experiences took a toll on the health and well-being of the family. I say this because, for a man or a woman, taking care of a family is coupled with great responsibility. My parents cared to provide us with the best living, education, and other needs without neglect; there were always new promises to keep and milestones to reach.

As Alfred Lord Tennyson says, "Man for the field and woman for the hearth."

During those days, women preferred to stay home to care for the larger families.

Giving birth and raising kids is not a woman's only responsibility; she provides them with the best upbringing, teaches morals, instills strong values, and balances many things in the family's interest.

Well! As a mother of two children today, while fulfilling my duties, I realize my mother and father's enormous efforts to provide us with the best. I am proud of my parents and siblings for all the assimilation and reciprocation of teaching and learning in the best spirit.

तिनका तिनका जोड़े चिड़िया बनाए घरोंदे, कभी खुशहाली तो कभी मायूसी

हर दिन का सूरज लाए कुछ नया अनोखा, सीख जो जोड़े रखे हमेशा ऐसी

Homes resemble nests, knitted straw by straw; in the face of bittersweetness,

unity is the mantra, the warm sunshine each day brings vigor, positivity, and devotedness!

My roots lie in the town that has produced many sons and daughters of the land working for the country and abroad in top positions across various fields. Although our town lacked specific amenities, it had reputed convent schools. Over time, few things changed, but the infrastructural shortcomings were apparent compared to other cities. In the past twenty-five years, numerous local political leaders took over the political reins, yet it is unendurable to witness only slight progress. As an ordinary citizen with little political insight, the deeper I delve into complex things, the naiver I am in understanding these dynamics.

दिल में बसे ख़ास मुक़ाम मेरे वतन मेरे गाँव के लिए,

देखना चाहे दिल इसे फलता फूलता,

तरक्की की तवक्को ऐसी सुनहरे ख्वाब बुनते

यह मुक़ाम हो सोने की चिड़िया का घरोंदा जैसे!

मगर अफ़सोस, दवा पढ़ाई और कई सहूलतों से महरूम, ढूँढ़ते रह गए रास्ते!

दौड़ लगाए शहर की ओर, बेगाने बेगाने ही रह गए सालों साल तरसते!

Hometown, the cradle, always close to heart, eyes longing to see it

Flourish like the nest of a golden bird, but alas, long wait! It left us deprived!

Better services, medicine, higher education, unfulfilled dreams of discontent

Alas! Strangers, we remained remote from services and progress for years!

My hometown has witnessed people relocating to nearby urban cities in search of better opportunities in education and employment, transportation, medicine, and many other fields. Enhancing these amenities within the town can prevent the exodus. There are many strange and challenging lessons to learn and unlearn. In collaboration with the government, the elite and like-minded with a shared vision can be committed to working for the town's growth with sheer hard work. Nevertheless, the disparity in developmental activity in my hometown left me bewildered until my recent visit, which led me to see some developmental changes. Considering its hidden wealth of resources, I hope more attention ensures the due growth for people of all strata deserved all these years. As a long-term resident, I earnestly wish for the dreams of my people to come true and see my hometown flourish as an ever-shining star.

मुल्क की तरक्की शहर से नहीं गाँवों से होनी चाहिए,

अनाज, फल, फूल गाँव की भीनी मिट्टी में ही हैं उगते,

कवि कलाकार भी गाँव के ही हैं होते जवाहरात

दुनिया की समझ भी शहर कम और गाँव ज्यादा हैं सिखाते

गाँव की मिट्टी में ही है होती ख़ुशबू ख़ुशनुमा नमी भरी,

हैं खेत खलिहान हरे भरे ख़ुदरत के रंग और नज़ारे लिए भरपूर,

गाँव में बसी है शहर कीआत्मा बिना गाँव हो जंगल कहाँ,

सारे खेत खलिहान सूने; अनाज, फल, फूल हो सब गुम जहाँ

Cities teach lessons on mechanical work, but the countryside is rich in worldly awareness!

The growth and success of the country is linked to towns more than cities!

Grains, fruits, and flowers thrive in moist village soil

Scores of artists and poets of fame, the shiny pearls emerge from village landscapes

Pleasant fragrance attests to village soil, agriculture, fruit, millets

glimpses of decoration and vibrant colors abound and enthrall nature!

During this time, challenges came knocking at our door in the form of different issues; some societal disturbances and pressures related to family health issues were grueling.

Life throws many challenging trials at every step, and you must encounter them with a pat on your shoulder and a courageous spirit, as, at times, you have no choice except to accept and face them. There are many instances where you stumble upon to realize that you are unfortunate and hit rock bottom. Whether you fall hopelessly or stand firm, facing the wind gales of storms, it is entirely upon you. Worry drains the mind, but all the difficulties and hardships one faces transform you into a better person in the long run. Such is the nature of life; it determines one's outlook on life!

Shakespeare very well said, "Sweet are the uses of Adversity."

Indeed, they are!

जीवन के रसूमात कई, कुछ नर्म तो कुछ सख्त

छोटे तूफ़ान भी छोड़ें घाव गहरे, बस संघर्ष ही है आइना जीत का हर वक़्त

समंदर की गहराई में मिलते सीप और मोती,

गर्मी और दबाव में तप कर ही करे हीरा अपने मूल्य की प्राप्ति

गिरना और उठना सिखाते हैं अनगिनत ज़िंदगी के सबक लगातार

कमज़ोर बैठे रहे सिर्फ सपने बुन, कामयाब उठे मजबूत और पकडे रफ़्तार

Let little storms not leave deeper wounds,

Struggles and triumphs are the ritual two sides of the coin of life,

Deep in the sea, oysters and pearls are found

To reveal its value, heat, and pressure, diamonds withstand!

Lessons of life are numerous, teach you to rise after a fall and be triumphant,

the stronger begets victory, while the weak rest in the sediment!

The role of a mother has a strong bearing on a family. My indebtedness grows multifold to my mother for giving me the best lessons of endurance, spirituality, and code of conduct. Her enriching book-reading sessions on general and spiritual subjects with all children nourished our minds and intensely influenced our thought patterns. As the oldest child, it was a richly rewarding experience. I closely followed her tone, and the readings had a symbolic inscription on my formative years; they tutored me to be a blessing to others in the most minute way possible! These lessons serve as an immense source of inspiration inscribed into my long-lived strong base for specific foundational values.

I strongly believe in adhering to one's roots; one may try new styles, but let the old classics remain your base with welcoming extensions as no complete topple-down. My favorite among the chapters Ammi (mom) read were from a book titled 'Adab e Zindagi,' a version in Urdu, my mother tongue, meaning 'Etiquettes of Life in Islam,' I imbibed the lesson in every word. These chapters guided me to be happy in my skin rather than trying to fit in borrowed or uncomfortable new cloaks. These phenomenal childhood experiences are still pristine and very close to my heart.

उन, ज्ञान और सीख भरी तालीम, किताबें पढ़ कर लफ़्ज़ों का मुआइने समझाना,

कैसे भूलूँ आप की आवाज़, तलफ़्फ़ुज़ और नर्म लहजे से मिलते पैग़ाम सही रोज़ाना

आत्म-अनुशासन के साथ समझौता न करने वाले पाठ आपके,

दिखाए राह नियम वाले, परज़ोर बोल आपके

ज़िंदगी के उतार चढ़ाव सिखाते सबक सीख वाले, जल्दबाज़ी से नहीं

बल्कि समझ, हिम्मत और हौसले से करें सामना, तजुर्बा है सिखाता यही

आपके सबक से हुई हर राह आसान बिना काँटा बिना संकोच

आपकी दी हुई सीख बने सबब ताज़गी का, जैसे चिराग रोशन जो जगाये उल्लास

How can I forget those book-reading sessions filled with knowledge and lessons?

Voice modulation precise, conveying the implied message!

Lessons on standing uncompromised with self-discipline,

treasure both ups and downs, as they carve you to face difficulty boldly,

Your lessons on life experience have brightened my days and life!

The freshness and happiness you filled in me are the beacon lights of my life!

Education as a catalyst expedites refinement and intellectual growth regardless of your scores and achievements. Additionally, a place of learning humbles you by providing knowledge, but wisdom and common sense are instrumental factors in its application. Refinement significantly reflects in one's behavioral patterns at home, school, or any other place of learning with friends, teachers, elders, relatives, and strangers. Intuitive learning goes beyond the degrees obtained from universities of great repute; one's openness to social sources matters most as learning at an in-depth level happens beyond a place of learning or through books—issues of everything contributing to making a better version of oneself. I believe that unbiased behavior towards the whole lot uplifts you and aids in seeking enlightenment and achieving inner peace and awareness.

The lessons I learned from my parents are beyond lessons learned in any school and college; they hold good even today and act as a manual of life as and when in need. They guide me towards a better understanding of life-related issues I encounter and seek solutions for. Thus, education, learning, and timely guidance from home can go a long way. This fine-tuned orchestration remains a guiding factor not for me alone but, over the years and for my seven other siblings, significantly impacting genetic and exposure aspects.

After many years, I now perceive my mother and father's characteristics as ingrained significantly in my siblings' physical appearance, gestures, features, smiles, mannerisms, and approaches toward life-related issues. Parents may or may not be physically present with us, but they leave chips of their blocks in some form, reminding us of their presence, escorting and steering us to the best, even from the heavens in the form of shining stars.

हर जज़्बे से है बड़ी माता पिता की सीख

साँझ सवेरे उन्ही के गूँजे गीत दो जहाँ में, कभी ज़मीन तो कभी फ़लक से,

ज़िंदगी में खींची हुई नर्म सख़्त रेखाओं में भी है दुआ,

नसीहत न्यारी जो सींचे हमें इतने प्यार और दुलार से

A Monumental stand, the lessons given by the parents in every sense!

May the song resonate in the morning and evening from the ground and the sky,

There lies a unique lesson of life in the boundaries drawn,

Blessed are you who nurtured us with so much love and affection!

1.3. RESPONSIBILITIES-ZIMMEDARI AS THE ELDEST DAUGHTER

(Commitment & Oneness)

Some situations disturb our peace of mind, and overthinking dominates only to amplify sadness. This entire experience contributed to my finding strength amidst times of unease. At the same time, I learned to stand firm and play different roles as a dutiful daughter, a responsible older sister, sometimes a moderator, and often a consoling factor, per the situation's requirements. However, my concern for my family was always at the forefront.

We went through a patchy phase of crisis related to my mother's health condition. I felt responsible and committed to my mother and siblings through thick and thin, even at a tender age. Taking care of younger siblings at certain appointed hours during inescapable emergencies was paramount, with self-care and other things in the backseat.

My close relatives, who watched me take up roles in my contribution to family matters, endorsed that I was wise and committed beyond my age in handling specific issues since childhood. At a later stage of life, it was a boon that I was rewarded and immensely blessed by the Almighty. I consider myself the favored oldest child; at least I was there for the family when it most needed me. I had to follow the golden rule to put up a courageous face and lead my younger siblings by holding their little fingers while walking the tightrope.

Eventually, responsibilities were relayed from one sibling to another in varying percentages! In the springtime of their lives, my siblings felt the obligation and showcased maturity beyond their age to handle many things. During these trying moments and always, my dad was the backbone and strong support for the entire family.

Every family goes through peaks and valleys of pressure, a mixture of good and bad domestic happenings. My family encountered frightening and scary nagging at home due to the needless meddling of kinsfolk; specific topics of contention cropped in and out. These disturbing situations led to deep psychological anguish for the entire family. But in all quietude, the wisdom in handling those moments and coping with the unwanted and the unwarranted stuff was a real challenge to us. Life's best moments to count on are when we stand by one another as one unit during distress.

There were days when my heart grew fonder of numerous enticements as a child towards typically playing games, eating street food, sulking, and being naughty as children my age. Still, life had different lessons for me and my siblings. We grew up to be more disciplined and engrossed in our thoughts and way of living; somewhere, these experiences demanded that my little siblings and I become more silent and observant.

बचपन ने सिखाई तहज़ीब, पहचान अच्छे बुरे वाली -सूझ बूझ भरपूर,

छोटे भाई बहन बने जान से प्यारे, ख़याल उनके हमेशा हर पल भर

सरपरस्त थे मात पिता, बावजूद इसके एक दुसरे का हाथ थामे ज़िम्मेदारी भरपूर

रिश्तेदार जन के अंदाज़ निराले कभी दख्ल ऐसे समझ न आने वाले पल भर

कभी लोरी तो कभी उदासी जैसे हर रुत बदले पल भर में

लगे दुनिया पैरों तले खिसकती कभी संवरते हालात तो कभी बिगड़ते

बादल गंभीर खौफनाक अँधेरा ऐसे डगमगाए कदम जैसे

दिशा तलाशते आगे बढ़ने वली, दिन बचपन के बीते सीख वाले,

Light of childhood innocence shines, younger siblings holding each other dearest,

Cautious of good and evil, drilling wisdom and responsibility abundant,

Under the shadow of love and care, tantrums of near and dear scare

Affectionate, complaining, and meddling sometimes, peace at stake

Desolate colors of woeful tempers blend with a lullaby of Halloween with frightening horror,

Worsened conditions, understanding the paramount requisite both for self and with others!

The sobbing moments escort clouds of scary darkness, with footsteps wobbling,

Lessons mastered through childhood remain unfading throughout!

My love for my siblings is boundless to date, and any small needle prick on my siblings makes me emotional. Even today, my thirty-year-old daughter, a girl with greater wisdom, makes fun of me, saying I love my siblings more than my children. I cannot deny how close they are to my heart. We all enjoyed making small sacrifices and adjustments for one another in the family without any complaints. However, the savored moments fill my heart with great happiness and fulfillment.

Though one appears happy-go-lucky, it isn't easy to understand that everyone goes through a journey of ups and downs unless highlighted or said aloud. As a girl in the -8year-old to teen bracket, my main point was understanding and adjusting to the perspective and standing by family members for greater contentment and rejoicing. It needs to step into others' shoes empathetically. But most of the time, some disturbances initially impact your inner peace, reflect upon personal growth, and intimidate your self-worth.

इंतज़ार उम्मीद लिए बदलते हालात के संवरने वाले

मजबूरी व बेबसी तोड़े कच्ची डाल, बने रुकावट फ़लने फूलने में

माँ बाप से है खायम ताक़त अमन और सुकून वाले

बिना इनके लगे हर मंच सूनाऔर हर आहट डर जगाने वाली

ज़िन्दगी के तूफ़ान में न बनो कश्ती बिना किनारे वाली

दुआ से सजे घर परिवार- बने घरोंदा आशियाँ ख़ुशियों वाला,

मुश्किल के पल में दिल खोजे राज़दार, दोस्त रिश्तेदार तो कई

आएंगे जताने हमदर्दी पर बिना हिचकिचाहट बुने मनगढंत कहानियाँ भी

Angels rest in the charming innocence of little ones, yearning for love, affection, and direction

seized in a whirlwind of circumstances, the whole world seems colorless,

Pressure and helplessness break a tender twig, eroding confidence

scared by every sound of the society, shattered by the storms of life,

In the bleakness in search of strength and support,

Young minds are broken and traumatized, and there is no one to console the broken hearts,

long with a wishful prayer for long-lasting laughter, peace, happiness,

After all, the dream of children dwells in the well-being of parents!

My experiences and interactions with my parents and maternal grandparents taught me to erase worrying habits, acknowledge disturbances, and find solutions. I learned to cope with specific mounting pressures in the initial stages. I felt a dire need to talk to someone. But little mind realized it was not sane, as it had a bouncing impact. People tend to probe into others' matters, add up tales, fan the flames, and present you in a bad light, leaving you baffled to realize when and how things went awry as a kid. A point comes when all the unpleasantness hurts, resulting in chaos and unproductiveness. Educational studies and other interests appear secondary as the family and kin will become your priority, to the extent that their minute health concerns or emotional crises are mounting to weigh you down. The consequences are seen in different dimensions. Interactions become limited, and circumstances turn you into a silent observer and a keen learner of life lessons that no great university teacher can impart.

Despite having enough resources and no financial constraints due to my dad's well-placed government job and sensible business investments, the weight of sporadic emotional struggles and some health crises overshadowed the harmonious family ties. Life appeared as a voyage without a compass; it led to inevitable disconnections, and the family searched for ways to cope with the stress, sometimes silently and sometimes through self-help strategies discovered by fumbling around in the dark.

These life lessons serve as case studies that offer more insights and hands-on experience. All these factors sparked greater insecurities, and countering them bolstered the confidence of my siblings and me, thus eliminating fears of ostracism. In the face of more significant worries, any other hurdle feels trivial; that's human psychology. You need a pragmatic approach to dealing with situations, which transforms you into the strongest person, and no worries can disturb you. It's when spiritual aspects emerge, and you start talking to God as your Confidant, the Provider, and the Sole Entity who can set things right. Eventually, there is a change in the caliber of thoughts; something that seemed unfair begins to clarify as you start to appreciate things and life in a better light. I understood the need to be practical and support others. Since childhood, my strategy during troubled times has been to talk positively to myself first and then look for the best ways to solve a problem without panic. Instead of fretting, I prepared myself to find the most straightforward solution by holding my ground firmly and emerging triumphant. What better way than this to learn life skills?

When destiny has chosen this way of teaching, will any other way of learning become preponderant?

मुश्किल के पल महसूस होने पर दिल खोजे राज़दार
किसी का गहना ऐतेबार हमदर्दी वाला तो किसी का ऐतेबार दिखावा ज़ोरदार

भोले बचपन का भी न हो लेहाज़, तोड़ मरोड़ बनाये फ़साने
आपका एक ही सहारा, ऐसे में,

परवरदिगारअपना राज़दारों का राज़दार

जो देखे सब कुछ, और सुने दिल की ख़ामोश पुकार

Agonizingly, many stand heartlessly diagnostic of family concerns,

But during challenging moments, the heart longs to seek a confidante!

Pretentious folks maneuver you scornfully,

disguised as sympathizers frame a fictitious story of empathy!

With zero care for the innocent buds of childhood,

hypocrites trick the formative minds. The only Caretaker, the Secret Keeper,

The Lord, the Protector, guards against impersonators,

Who sees everything and responds to the heart's sighs!

My mother was a little easygoing person with solid values; she shared many experiences from her childhood days and motivated us all to be go-getters. She used to say there is no point in sitting down unwisely and crying over spilled milk, but try with a focused mind for a better next moment! My disciplinarian father taught us to be agile and not to have a laid-back attitude. I learned some real-life lessons from my grandmother, too. Unlike my mother, my grandmother did not attend high school but was rich in life experiences; she was strict in discipline; she used "Muhavre," meaning "sayings/idioms in English." I can never forget her lesson on being careful with words; she used to say, 'Zubaan se nikli hui baat aur kaman se nikla hua teer wapas nahi le sakte' Meaning 'Words once spoken, like an arrow from a bow, cannot be recalled' and also the Urdu version of 'Cut your coat according to the cloth.' These have been my life lessons so far, which have taught me to be committed to values and morals, embrace the sayings and preaching of my elders, and have deep faith in the Supreme Power. There comes a significant turning point in everyone's life for a better tomorrow.

William Shakespeare's Quote: "And this our life, exempt from public haunt, finds tongues in trees, books in the running brooks, sermons in stones, and good in everything," reminds me to be open to learning by all means.

कैसे भूलें माँ तुम से जो मिली सीख ऐसी उसूलों वाली

ना डरने वाली लगन और जी जान से मुश्किल का सामना करवाने वाली

बाबा के वो संस्कार क्रम शिक्षण वाले, मिज़ाज में बरते सख़्ती ऊपरी

करवाए तमीज़ अच्छे बुरे की और सिखाए आँसू है कमज़ोरी की निशानी

नानी के बोल याद दिलाने वाले, "थामे रखो जुबान, है यह फसाद की जड़ का सामान"!

फुप्पी के इबादत में लगने में है हर मर्ज़ की दवा मानो, जैसे थम जाए हर तूफ़ान

कैसे भूलें माँ बाबा आप की तालीम है बसी हमारे रूह में

मिठास भरे वो ना भूलने वाली यादें जो समाये सारे पल बने आज तक की यादें

Mom, your lessons on dedication and living life without fear, immemorial,

And papa's values on acceptable behavior and discipline assimilated strongly,

Lessons on Judiciousness, tears, and sobbing signs of weakness

Firmness and challenges add up to your strength, said Dad,

Grandmother's advice on the indiscreet talk, the root of chaos,

Prayer and worship bring peace of heart, medicine for every ailment

Hold on to rules and principles; every storm eventually passes

There are many lessons to learn; every instance comes with a moral!

1.4 FILLING THE GAPS: EDUCATION, FRIENDS, TEENAGE-EXPECTATIONS

I owe a lot to the town and convent missionary school; it was a boon to help me learn and nurture the best. My school experiences filled my childhood with fun coupled with learning. We learned to be disciplined, adaptable, and focused on our studies. We filled many gaps and grew in a fresh environment while spending time with friends and honing our communication skills.

School teachers and nuns were crucial in directing pupils towards goal setting and achieving them. Despite this facility, my early years were an aimless approach, with less self-awareness. I was primarily shy and a silent girl with reasonably good academic performance. Without pressure on behavior patterns, lessons to collaborate with peers and understand self-worth were loud and clear. I am unsure if it was goals or ambitions that motivated me. However, some nestled thoughts in the shadows often led to disappointing tracks. I ponder whether some unforgettable incidents and troublesome things made me reflective and reticent.

पाठशाला के शिक्षक, दोस्त जो साथ हैं और जो नहीं यादगार सारे

किन किन को याद करें हम, ना भूलने वाली मिठास भरी यादें!

ये दोस्त भी ऐसे जो हर दिन एक बहाना ढूंढे सारी यादें ताज़ा करने वाले

खेल कूद ऐसे मनमोहने वाले खुद को संभालने वाले सारी फ़िक्र गुम करने वाले

Reflecting on moments from childhood till today, school, teachers, friends

the more you remember, the sweeter sound those unforgettable memories

Friends for fun, teachers for lessons, corrections, and morals too

Time spent in sports and games so captivating, evade any fear or woe

Friends who find an excuse every day to refresh all memories

Sweet evocations of reminisce that cherish forever!

However, the fire incident during my initial schooling years left deep confusion in my siblings' and my mind for a long time.

The troubling effects and intense influence of the entire incident weighed heavily on my father for a long time. Nevertheless, he tried his best to unravel the sadness and erase that trauma from our minds by taking us on a vacation to Bombay (presently known as Mumbai) and Ooty. Despite his efforts, the traumatic experiences would haunt us occasionally.

Fortunately, the mind is a sieve, and time is the best healer. Specific memories fade gradually, and we try to learn and adapt to new changes and surroundings, but the indentations remain.

Life experiences contribute significantly to learning life lessons. In my case, I was blossoming in that aspect subconsciously. Undeniably, school teachers are accredited at such stages to motivate and transform students. I imbibed a lot from my teachers, who role-modeled us through behavior, approach, style, and many other ways of instilling values and cultivating eagerness. Along with regular academics, acquiring required skills and nurturing skill-driven repositories led to my refinement.

Expertise comes from evaluation and dedication; I'm still determining an evaluation; however, dedication is significantly linked to my Ammi, as her words were richly motivating. Out of respect for her, I aimed to be the most dedicated in completing any assigned task. I might have applied it better to the hilt towards my education and career building, but it was abundant in other household matters, assisting Ammi.

The challenging period during my high school escalated; destiny had different plans, life took painful turns, and things came to a standstill. Perhaps the mayhem of the car fire accident and a couple of quivering incidents had a profound effect on the silent theater of my mother's mind, turning her into a ruffled soul, and eventually she encountered ill health.

My mother was constantly under trials and tribulations due to her health issues; seeing her in pain and anguish was all the more unbearable for my seven siblings and me. My dad was of constant support, no doubt, but he had more things to deal with: his work, eight children to take care of, an ailing wife with whom he had spent a quality life, and focus on plans for a future settled life ahead for the entire family.

At this point, a turbulent chapter began in our life. My grandfather fell sick; her father was a world to my mother; she loved him dearly and started worrying for him over her suffering. Consequently, her health started deteriorating faster. Watching my mother, who was my strength in distress, was heart-wrenching. The mellifluous voice of my mom calling us for breakfast, lunch, and dinner started becoming feeble.

God is merciful in giving us many bountiful possessions. Apart from family, friends are significant assets who hold your hand; a gentle pat with love and care remains magical among all the prized possessions during turbulence. To name a few, it would be unfair to the rest. I am deeply indebted to all my friends and relatives for being my guiding stars, companions, and towers of strength at various times of crisis.

Throughout my teenage years, I struggled with a gigantic inner battle; my mother's ailment left us devastated. After a series of health shortfalls, starting gradually and resulting in frequent painful, unhealthy spells over six years, my mom was deteriorating day by day, health-wise and appearance-wise. A hopeless, gloomy, weak appearance replaced her vibrant, healthy look. The lifelessness overpowered her entire body, her voice became weak day by day, her strength pulled down, and she needed assistance for eating and attending to other chores, especially for the later stages of her life.

Despite knowing that she had a very short period of life left and the end was fast approaching, my Ammi tried hard to put up a heroic face and fight it in her solitude without giving up hope, nor did she express displeasure to the Supreme Power about her early calling. My Ammi never voiced dissatisfaction or anguish for the young kids she would leave behind. She kept herself strong, overcoming her internal brawls, possibly through her spirituality. I often saw her reciting some verses of the Quran, which was the best she could do. For me, seeing her strong even in such moments of emotional crisis was a tricky thing then.

She was an embodiment of spiritual strength and inner peace. My dear mom was intense and very much iron-willed; even on her deathbed, she cared for people around her and their well-being by ensuring they ate meals on time and got needed rest. Even in the last worrisome days, she was keen on meeting family members with a welcoming smile and a caring tone; her boundless affection for everyone, even for non-family members, makes her stand out. It puts us all to enormous pangs of suffering to remember her painful days and the untold agony she withstood over time. Her memories are always with us in the best of forms, but for a reason not to bring tears to other family members, it remains a silently felt but undiscussed topic in the family. And the most pathetic of what one could imagine, or dread to see one's mom in such a state! We had no courage to see our dear mother in that helpless state!

Alas! We finally landed on the destined unfortunate day! A doomsday for the family, at least for that time. My mom was residing at my grandmother's house due to severe illness for a couple of days; one gloomy evening, it was an inner call for all of us that prompted us to gather unplanned. Our family members visited her anxiously. But that unforgettable evening, looking at her pale and weak body, I experienced an unknown fear filled with desolation. The time was almost twilight, that of maghrib prayers; I was holding my seven-month-old daughter in my arms, and my mother looked at me, saying, "How is the baby? Take care. She must be hungry. All of you go home. Eat your supper, and you can come again later." Those were the last words uttered for us. We reached home and had supper; we were immediately asked to return to grandma's place, owned by my father, only to know that we had lost her forever; my second sister and my grandma were by her side during that appointed last hour.

My father, waiting outside, was the most shattered person, losing his life partner of twenty-five years and a big family to take care of, broken and shaken from within yet trying to do the needful in arranging her last journey and standing as a pillar of strength for the family was another deplorable situation to watch for anyone.

Her last journey to the kabristan (the burial ground), the poorest of our emotional bankruptcy moment, is still fresh in my memory; the entire process of ablution (giving a bath to her body) enshrouded her in the white shroud, which is called kafan, her hair wrapped up and head covered in the 'aurni,' the headband, was the most beautiful and memorable impression. The noor (radiance) with which her face illuminated that day is beyond expression. As she was taken away to the mosque for the janaza prayers, the light clouds and drizzling added to the somberness that day, the fifth of January 1994. Life is a precious gift, but what we take with us is the goodness with a bit of place in others' hearts for our 'aamaal' (conduct). People greatly loved her, and she always left an unforgettable impression on those she met.

ख़ौफ़ अनजाना तुम्हारे बिछड़ने का था दिल में छुपा, अचानक से आई हवा तूफानी

हुआ टूटा एक तारा गुमशुदा और शाख़ें दरख़्त की जैसी बिखर सी गई

तम्हीं पर सारी मुसलसल आस थी टिकी तुम ही सदाबहार जीने का था सहारा

ख़ुशियों का सिलसिला मुख़्तसर, मानो थम सी गयी सारी दुनिया

Hidden fear of separation haunted from within suddenly swept a stormy wind,

A star fell with gloom unending, scattered branches lay withered,

moments of happiness, short-lived!

Came to a standstill, our blissful little world

The ray of our life, all hopes on you pinned,

needed to start afresh with broken wings, our world seemingly conquered!

My friends recall the hardships my mom and the family faced during those days and how we stood firm to overcome the gloomy days with tearful eyes. These reminders send shivers down my spine.

There was no other choice except to face the pathetic, deplorable situation at home; well, the support of my extended family, both my maternal and paternal sides, was much needed and highly appreciated.

I sincerely acknowledge the unforgettable support of my neighbors next door during that difficult time. God bless them. As kids, whenever we needed them, their kind gestures of volunteering help without hesitation always touched our hearts. The only way to reciprocate is to keep them in our dua and pray for their happiness and well-being.

When I think of those saddening moments, the brutal, excruciating pain that we went through then and the trauma of every family member crosses my mind. As a family, we could only drown in the choices of desperation but could do little. However, considering several factors, the wise approach to the need of the hour was to put back the broken pieces of devastating loneliness, and we had to demonstrate outward projection of strength and consolation for one another; these moments of life come with more incredible lessons which no book teaches, one needs to be courageous to put back a smile and head towards normalcy.

Tough times come as the most brutal blows and as a test of one's personality; life's best lessons are to endure with patience and vigilance by being balanced even during trying hours. My encounter with varied situations brought me closer to people's ordeal in terms of family unrest, emotional crises, and abuse of various types. Some morbid catastrophes people suffer made me empathetic towards society and its evils, understanding one's vulnerability to internal struggles. These instances disciplined me to be concerned and understand the frail moment when people succumb to pain, certain abuses, and evil practices. Sensibility and magnanimity lie in being unbiased in exercising special care, better understanding, mercy, and respect toward others.

When I sit alone and collect my thoughts, one question that slowly creeps into my mind is, who are we to be judgmental and draw barriers to choices? However, the thin dividing line needs to be appreciated by all means; otherwise, it can be a mere defense line drawn to fulfill unjust ambitions of greed and division. How one deals with personal crises is to be emphasized, as things may take miserable turns irrationally, and mishandling leads to worse anxiety and depression. Spiritual strength and sacredness can be crucial while dealing with such issues.

घाव, कई, कुछ कच्चे तो कुछ भरे से, सच में है एक इम्तिहान यह जिंदगी

एक हल्की सी आहट जगाए उम्मीद की किरण, एक दिया जैसे भरे उमंग रोशनी वाली

तकलीफ़ों के भंवर में डूबे ए परेशान ज़दा दिल, खुद ही को तैर कर है तट पर जाना

और संभलना, माज़ी को छोड़ अकलमंदी है फ़िलहाल आज ही में जीना

उजली किरण की उम्र हो कम काले बादल जैसे घिरे तूफ़ानी अंधेरों में

उठना है बुलंद तुम्हीं को, हर थामा हुआ हाथ खैरख़्वाह का न हो जानलें

इस में कोई फ़र्ज़ी भी हो शामिल, भले ही आँख मूँदे रखो,

सतर्क रहना है ज़रूरी जिंदगी के कई सबक गाँठ बाँध के

Many wounds, some raw, some healed, life is truly a test!

A faint sound of footsteps can awaken a ray of hope, like a tiny lamp in the dark tempest!

In the light of excitement or the whirlpool of troubles, alertness is the key,

Rise and learn to fight; brightness is short-lived, and life's journey is not easy!

Despite the dark bad storms, every hand that reaches you may not be a helping one!

In a whirlwind, one must dare to swim to the shore alone!

Susceptibilities to fakeness and deceptiveness need alertness,

Even if you keep your eyes closed, let your conscience stay watchful,

Be awakened to life lessons; they teach us to walk out of a cage of bewilderment,

Life is not easy, but attempt to make it easy and great!

Having said this, handling success and failure in life, maintaining composure, and making moments memorable is entirely up to you. Others can guide you, but your decisions and acknowledgment of the service rendered at various stages make the best of you. These small gestures of gratitude take you a long way.

As we examine these choices, we find that they also depend on one's circumstances, mindset, and expectations in different situations, including the parent-child relationship, personal experiences, childhood, adulthood, relationships, and society at large; accordingly, thought processes throughout are significant aspects of dealing with deeper learning.

There are many life lessons: the sooner you come to terms with them, the better you can devise your coping strategies. The canvas of life is not always as you expect; life comes with so many twists and turns, and problems hurt and shake people. It takes you to euphoric highs and sometimes brings shocks and surprises to knock you down; we need to learn to stand firm and chase the pleasures of life.

जीवन पसंदीदा चमकीले रंगों से रंगा जाने वाला एक चित्र फलक है,

पर हर तसव्वुर का गहरा ज़रिया ख़ुदा की कायनात में छिपा है

मन को नसीहत मिले, मुख्तलिफ ख़याल हो मज़बूत गहरायी वाले,

मुख्तलिफ रूप ले आये नतीजे, जब हो ख़यालात हिम्मत अफ़ज़ाई वाले

Life is a canvas to be filled with vivid colors of choice,

Profound imaginative perfection, the source

A deeply engrossed mind directs a variety of deliberations

Perception, as the catalyst, results in distinctness in shapes!

SIBLINGS-RELAY OF RESPONSIBILITIES

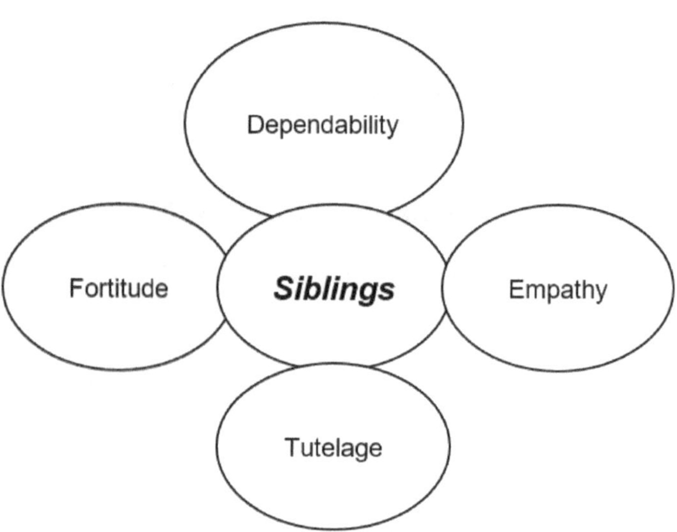

The calmest seas will have traces of the deadliest, most disturbing storms, and also beautiful corals, gems, and pearls are found underneath the muddy layers.

Similar was the situation after the loss of my mother for the entire family when times were tough. As a single parent, my father tried to pull the bits together. He stood firm as an emotional strength for the family and as a virtuous asset. Despite his guidance and all kinds of support, as an older sibling, seeing seven of my siblings between the age group of eighteen and five years struggling with their chores was nothing but navigating through uncharted waters, and it was a heart-wrenching thing for me. However, the care and concern of a few nearest relatives were instrumental in times of need.

Even otherwise, in the presence of both parents, the older siblings become guides to lead the younger ones by hand; this act develops a stronger bond of reverence among siblings at later stages of life. At the onset of unforeseen circumstances of losing one parent, the older siblings take on a parenting role, and in our case, all of my siblings relayed it. However, it was challenging for my younger siblings to adjust to the new setup, caring for one another without the mother as an anchor; destiny's harsh trials replaced their smiles and laughter with a thorny path.

Such experiences led to emotional upheaval and adjustment issues among siblings, occasionally leading to a few disagreements and internal conflicts. Careful analysis and optimism helped us all mellow down and downsize the trauma through love and care, resorting to prioritizing and conceptual changes.

As an older sister, my profound affection towards my younger siblings has been like delving into an ocean of unfathomable love. Ultimately, circumstances master you in the best lessons of life. We all learned the art of collecting broken pieces and appeared strong outside, though we were weak and crying within. The unforgettable painful memories, sickness of our mother, and coping with the loss filled our hearts with unceasing kindness forever for a reason.

I closely observed my mother's soft spot and concern for orphans throughout her life. At such hours of distress, the thought of her concern always lingered, and even today, it's very heart-wrenching to see young kids struggling without parents. Numerous factors helped us remain calm and mellow down and stand by ourselves during those days of struggle. We believed that being strong and taking care of one another would put her soul to rest peacefully. My younger siblings had to strive hard to come to terms with all the acclimatization in life. Undergoing crawling pain in ignorance and caring for it all alone was challenging at that tender age.

However, initially, the little fact of the wilderness of confusion was in flow; crying, brawling, arranging, and rearranging could not be ignored among siblings. At times, things would get on our nerves, but with a worthwhile strictness, tender craving, and a hunt to drive each other crazy, many silly activities would be attempted to pull on one another; all these acts resulted in my siblings' togetherness. We all helped one another with all cooperation to fade away strings of sadness, ensuring a sweet, emotional, faint laugh.

राह दिखाए ऊँच नीच भी समझाए वजूद रिश्ते नातों का, आस भी बनाए

नासाज़गी, दर्द, तकलीफ, जुदाई में भी जीने का मतलब है सिखाए,

करे बयान मासूमियत हार जीत या दर्द, झलकते अंदाज़ इनके ना जाने अपने पराए

बिना अल्फ़ाज़ कहते हैं बहुत कुछ, ऐ यादगार पल, तुम पर हज़ारों आंसु क़ुर्बान

Create new pathways and marshal the way, decode the existence of relationships,

Connotations of living are taught even in the face of insensitivity, pain, and discomfort!

Innocence in expression, victory, defeat, or pain, all patterns identical, but voicing hushed,

Alas, I shed thousands of tears in memorabilia for you!

Gradually, my siblings began to share experiences, visit me, play games, discuss movies, resort to humor, hide fights, and spread love.

Indulging in funny attempts with coded faces resulted in laughter, and the fragrance of stronger bonding unfolded to sing softly, sweeping sighs aside.

During my frequent visits, I noticed the young children, engulfed in the shackles of loneliness due to the tragic loss of our mom, found ways to regulate a great bond among themselves. They helped each other in all homely chores, cooking, cleaning, getting ready for school, tying ribbons to plaits and fastening shoelaces, and packing lunch boxes to school for some time with a baton of responsibilities shifting from one sibling to the next as per age with deeper connections.

Later, my dad engaged a cook to ease household chores. However, I was just a call away for sharing and guidance. We frequently communicated about health matters, daily requirements, and cooking procedures. Even today, after thirty years, my sisters fondly remember sharing simple things that used to happen and the phone calls they made to me to confirm the steps of pre-cooking and cooking.

My father served as the anchor and my siblings focused on nurturing stronger bonds. Over time, the children started understanding that one needs to overcome empty noise through unconditional love. Each one had to shoulder the parental role towards younger siblings coming their way one by one.

Nonetheless, witnessing the blend and traces of traits in siblings inherited from both parents in behavior, resemblances, expressions of joy, frowns, wisdom, adaptations in life, and swiftness in dealing with many anxious situations creates more profound connections. The best of bequeathal left behind as footprints in the sand of time represent memories of purest love.

My seven siblings are like angels to me; we all grew up together at different stages of life, disguised as the thickest friends from the same womb. When I look at their faces, memories of childhood sharing, caring, playing, and naughtiness flash at a thunderous speed. Our sense of responsibility was like a thread that entwines all the goodness of a family's ornamentation.

Over thirty years after my mother, it is overwhelming to note that my seven siblings have become independent adults. They have acquired higher educational qualifications, placed well in their careers, and settled down in their married lives. Of course, the journey was not always rosy, but they were resilient to changes and emerged triumphant in all domains.

What best would life give us?

Shukran ya Rab

A big thanks to the Almighty!

टिमटिमाती रौशनी लिए आँखों में याद है मुझे माँ का फख़्र से कहना

मेरे दो बेटे चाँद सूरज जैसे, बाबा का कहना आबाद रहे घर अपना बेटियों से

जैसे बाग़ और बगीचा हरा भरा, नाज़ुक पंखुड़ी वाले पुष्प उपवन के

छोटे बड़े, इन्द्रधनुष सी सतरंगी मुस्कान बिखेरे

With twinkling shiny eyes and pride, my mother

describes her sons as the moon and the sun,

Baba's hope for a prosperous home resembling a mesmerizing garden,

with vibrant flowers spreading smiles like arrays of rainbow colors

बहनों और भाइयों के अच्छे बंधन दरख़्त -वृक्ष जैसे, मज़बूत छाया,

शरारत और घबराहट के बावजूद फल फूल का लिए रूप एकजुटता से खड़े रहना,

कुछ धुंधलाते विचार के बादल भी घिरते कभी, तो कभी सहना सहमना,

कभी प्यार दुलार से एक ट्रसरों की तकलीफ समझना, कभी इंतज़ार चमत्कार का करना!

Standing in solidarity with the mischief and trepidation,

siblings finding security in love like mighty trees sharing fruit and blossoms

Together, we stand with all messy crew of hazy deliberations to be resolved,

from naughtiness and bewilderment to moments of joy filled with fragrances,

परिवार मेरा हो जब एक चमन समान माँ बाप बन माली सींचें जिसे

कोमल बेल फल फूल हो बहन भाई,चमकदार चाँद सूरज संग आसमाँ तले

है अपनी अपनी पसंद किसी की फूल तो किसी की बेल,

और मेरी है फूलों में पसंद ताज़े ताज़े फूल भीनी सुगंध वाले लिली के

If a family resembles a garden, then my parents, the gardeners,

my siblings, like flowers—some gentle and others bright like the sun and moon,

We all have our preferences; some adore blooms, while others favor vines,

My personal favorite stand, the pleasantly scented fresh lily blossoms!

सुन्दर नीले आकाश के छाते तले मात्रुता और पित्रुता के अनुराग में समाये आठ जन, अपनी अपनी शख़्सियत लिए!

Under the umbrella of the lovely azure sky, sheltered by the warmth of parental love

Eight children, each with their unique personality, consistently remain steadfast

My second sibling,

Amidst fogs of hazy vision, precious eyes discern vices and virtues!

Patience is plenty laced with love, affection, and care!

चन्द्रमा सी कोमलता ढेर सारा धैर्य और सब्र लिए मेरे भाई की दो विशेषताएं

दो आंखें हो ऐसे न्यारे भला भी बुरा भी, हर नज़ारा समाए इनमें गहरी छाप लिए

My brother, the second child in the family, is a generous person with abundant brotherhood; he spreads happiness, friendliness, and immense strength even when battling sickness. Despite solidarity, he is put to trials and tests in the pitiful nest, faded under the wreckage of fragile expressions of love and concern. He is thoughtful of others. However, the pain still becomes apparent when one is intimidated and sometimes teased by the situations and destiny during which the sweetest bonds of appreciation sink in quicksand. However, he is an active listener, strangely patient and forgiving and caring even during the advent of hard times.

My third sibling, the beautiful shamrock with three petals.

अगली तीन पंखुड़ियों वाली सुंदर शेमरॉक सी प्यारी, बहन मेरी

With faith, hope, and love, her strength lies in the beauty and the sweetness of expression of love and care that became her signature traits, which include giving warm hugs and showering the children in the family with affectionate kisses. The accumulated unhidden pain bursts in spells as a volcano, at times of distress and helplessness, with momentary ease in the form of tears. She is strong willed with immense compassion, generosity, and strong intuitions. Her undeniable fondness lies in touching others' hearts as a juvenile entertainer with childlike expressions; her extreme thoughtfulness toward others is commendable. She is strongly driven by passion and honesty as a jewel, with a patient lending of an ear as strength to the core.

The next sibling lucky clover with four petals at number four

बहन मेरी चार पंखुड़ी वाली भाग्यशाली तिपतिया घास या गुल फ़्रन्जानि है जैसे

My mother's favorite child, assertive and straightforward, resorts to a positive attitude toward life, has zero tolerance for nonsense, and prefers a disciplined approach to life. The genuine concern lies in realizing her presence to regulate inside craving by standing shoulder to shoulder at times of worn-out, scary battles—sensitive, ever-conscious, punctual, and expert in detailing. Creativity is a trademark blessed with the ability to laugh at situations and herself, adding a fantastic touch of humor at times of adversity. She was born with the courage to handle situations laced with panic easily.

Number five signifies five senses, sometimes smooth and otherwise indistinct, warm and cold, my youngest brother

अंक पांच पांच इंद्रियों का प्रतीक है, कभी सय्यम, कभी नरम कभी अस्पष्ट,
तो कभी गर्म और कभी ठंडा छोटा भाई मेरा

He is practical in handling things but has inner fragility and humility, a very bold and robust external style, and a little stubborn outlook sometimes. He is affectionate in understanding tedious leaps and stands for others. He is not a people pleaser often but focuses on financial security, with clear lessons on accountability in economic matters. He never shies from climbing the constant, heavily burdened measures of fantasy. His strong and assertive style sometimes turns out to be blunt; he focuses on goals with clarity and openness as an understanding of creativity.

The next one is like a lily with six petals
अगली आए छह पंखुड़ियों वाली लिली हो बारीचे की जैसे
बहन मेरी थोड़ी से नर्म तो थोड़ी से अटल

She is a hard worker, a go-getter, a financial planner, scrupulous in handling things, an expert in connecting dots, and strong in gut feeling. She is assertive in style, has a stern approach, and looks enclosed with a ginger smile, but softness within adds kindness to her kitty. She never hesitates to call a spade a spade. Some life lessons taught her the significance of courage and care, and she excels in concealing stuff to unfold required information as needed. The trials of her life led her to steadfastness and a positive attitude towards life.

The next one like a star flower adorns a beautiful seven-colored smile of a rainbow
इंद्रधनुष की खूबसूरत सात रंगों वाली मुस्कुराहट लिए चक्रफूल सी यह लड़की

Crisp and concise, her wisdom, creativity, and out-of-the-box thinking are unique. She is blessed with a priceless possession of quick adjustments and an understanding of anything. Thoughtful to get along well as a great friend. She is a composed speaker and a patient listener. Over time, she learned the endearing traits to earn the wings of smiles through restless scars of tears; she mastered fluttering her wings in kindness to others. Further, she is as soft as a feather at heart with a distinct poise and never crosses limitations of approach in conversations. Frankness and forgiveness are her seals.

The loveliest lotus with eight petals, all unique on her own the youngest!

और आठ पंखुड़ियों वाली जैसे कमल के गुण लिए जो अपने आप है अनोखी

She can form the sweetest of bonds but drift apart at times in the shackles of perfection—the most affectionate and likable of all. A style queen deemed to be a shopaholic. An ever-smiling girl, often dressed to the nines, clings to sentiments resulting in crazier outcomes. It keeps humming, the remnants of loneliness of the past pulled into the present, winged with hopes and dreams. Open to trying new things, she has an edge over the leg-pulling of older siblings with her bubbly, cheerful style, and sometimes, her seriousness is taken easy, owing to her concealed jovial nature, capable of leaving a positive impression on others. She is a grown-up child but continues forever with her unpretentious temperament of a teenager.

"The strongest principle of growth lies in the human choice."– George Eliot.

The relay of responsibilities and the waves of life taught us that the convoy of life is not always smooth; one must learn to embrace the bumpy path and seek innovative ways to transform a rough, patchy trail into a rewarding one. Life's beauty lies in enduring ups and downs with courage; no one understands what one is going through. Every action defines a person, and life imparts vital lessons to push aside bitterness and strive hard to overcome difficulties with fortitude. As a bird does, one should pull courage and stand up to draw the twigs and hay to build one's own nest. Life's pendulum swings in two directions. Without experiencing pain, how do we appreciate the happiness we receive?

We meet many people in life, and everyone has a unique role; everything shifts if we embrace change and remain open to learning. Life is all about how we improvise ourselves each day. The world around us doesn't need our riches or a helping hand in that regard; the only requisite is a positive, cheerful approach, a warm smile that can alleviate any stress, and this can be infectious to spread joy within circles around you, certain moments taught me that 'silence speaks louder than words.' A hopeful mind never relinquishes optimism and keeps one moving forward.

जिंदगी का कड़वा सच मानो या ना मानो है बदलाव

अगर हम कुछ पल भूल कर आगे ना बढ़ पाए

तो रुकावट वाला सन्नाटा छाए

खुद को करें बुलंद इतना के छू ना पाए कोई तनाव

बेबसी कमियों वाली करवाए एहसास ये तन्ज़िया मुस्कान

लड़ाई जब खुद ही से हो तो डट कर करें मुकाबला, बुलंद हो पहचान,

तकलीफ में साए से भी ना टकराए तनाव

मज़बूत इरादों के आगे मामूली लगे हर मुश्किल या गहरे घाव

The truth of life lies in change, which is inevitable,

Sporadic twists, tosses, and turns sway you hither thither!

Life would not be accessible if forgetfulness were not a boon or time a healer

Keep moving forward in strength, even in trials, by lifting yourselves higher and higher!

Let no difficulty collide even with your farthest shadow

This damn snigger, ready to tease ridiculously even in difficulties

Work such that your identity soars high, to face every difficulty bravely,

May your lofty intentions make every complexity seem trivial!

FAMILY & KIDS

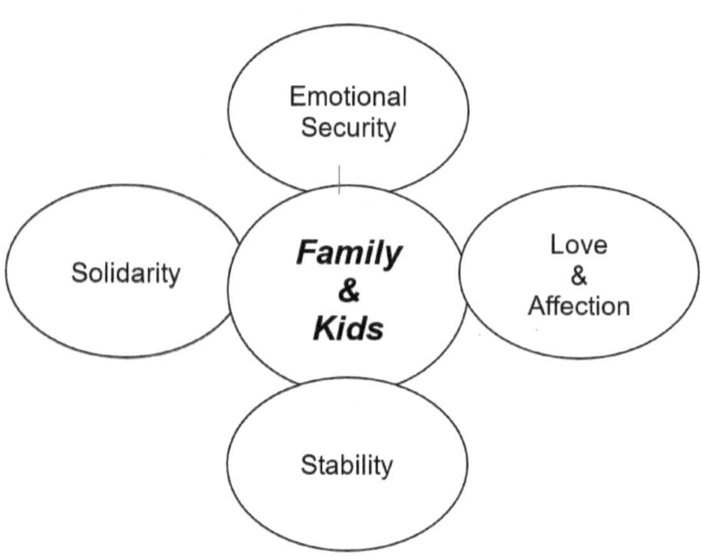

3.1 GIRLS THE PITCHERS OF SACRAMENTAL BONDS

"Courage, sacrifice, determination, commitment,
toughness, heart, talent, guts.

That's what little girls are made of."

– Bethany Hamilton.

I have always cherished my identity as a woman and believe in honoring womanhood with the utmost positivity and respect. My close observation of my mother and other women in the family and neighborhood has always filled me with awe at how a woman is a blessing with unexhausted magic catering to the needs of people around her. As a provider of new life and growth, a woman nurtures and impacts lives with her unique identity. The Supreme Power has bestowed feminine qualities upon many of His marvelous creations, showing the Almighty's commitment to safeguarding and blessing women with special attention.

The urban and rural Indian society is rich in cultural diversity, with lifestyle preferences, education, sports, understanding of raising kids, and adaptability to modernization. Women and young girls are treated as torchbearers of traditions and cultures, creating the rich fiber of a society by building healthily nurtured homes with a solid foundation; however, in the multiplex fabric of society and the prevalent pressure threads that run through girls' lives, discipline and tune them for pre-defined roles. Such portrayal in the name of societal acceptance generates a fortress of scrutiny, subjecting young girls to inner conflicts. Still, society understands them to be part of traditions and norms.

The panoramic view of marriage in Indian society before and during the 1980s and 1990s was typical. Early marriage talks would significantly make rounds at homes since girls attain the age of fifteen; the turmoil under the suffocating stereotypes and stigmatization would set aside talent and career, depressingly impacting young girls. Pathetic traces of vulnerabilities in nutrition, self-care, and higher education enveloped women in the whispering whirlwinds of malaise as silent sufferers caught in a vicious cycle of disparity, jeopardizing their self-esteem and morale. However, a few families remained immune to such succumbing, encouraging girls to continue their education and pursue careers after marriage.

जितने लोग उतनी बातें गाँव शहर का अंतर लिए

कितनी उम्मीदों पर खरी उतरे लड़कियां

लिए कई अरमान और आर्जू ससुराल में नए

कभी बसने की चिंता तो कभी ख़याल नया घर बसाने वाले

माँ बाप की नसीहत और सीख रुसुमात वाली

रुखसती डोली में, और लड़की हुई परायी

ससुराल को है मानना घर अपना, खुद का एक जो था घरोंदा

जिस को थे समझे आशियाँ अपना, वह भी हुआ पराया

Many expectations for the girls to live up to!

Secondly, her desires and wishes are worrisome, settling in a new house,

And setting up a new, urban-rural divide with differing customs and traditions.

Into the bargain, the advice and lessons from the parents!

On considering in-laws' place as your home, then on

Alas, I stand a stranger in my own nest, my home!

Lamentably, the past generational divide sickeningly engulfs a part of society with deep-rooted patriarchal huts of history, hindering young girls at blooming stages by captivating their freedom in the guise of societal standards of acceptability.

However, the flagstone to marital bliss drapes the familial duties and responsibilities unique to the role of a daughter-in-law, an observation I drew intimately from the experiences of my kin, including my aunts and cousins who had a tightrope walk in a few instances under scrutiny. In some families, young couples face reservations about talking to each other in the presence of in-laws. Married girls have restrictions even to meet parents, and some families insist on women eating after the men in the family do; sitting in front of elders of the family is taboo within the family norms, and table manners and much more are under surveillance.

Until I started taking Gender Sensitization classes for engineering students, I had not given much thought to women's worldwide challenges due to conventions, customs, and notions of honor.

The unwanted paradigm of harsh expectations originated from the annals of time and is responsible for biases towards daughters in the name of societal standards and grooming. Every household knits a fragile framework for girls, imparting lessons with heavy expectations from a young age. The poem "Girl,[2]" written in 1978 by Jamaica Kincaid, aptly resonates with the narration of universal truth and the pressure to train young girls for future roles as wives, mothers, and daughters-in-law under the pretext of acquiring an acceptable behavioral code, left for girls as a futile battle to conquer intangible fears with the shackles of burdensome conventions. It reminds me of the subtle teachings of my grandmother, underscoring societal expectations during my childhood.

The elements of nature, Mother Earth, and the rivers are feminine references. They encounter bouts of ebbs and flows as natural phenomena yet retain vitality through calmness, signifying newness in life. Similarly, women sculpt in the fresh aromas of caregiving with endurance and overcome any desolate situation with calmness and a gentle smile.

---

2   Tearle, Oliver. A Summary and Analysis of Jamaica Kincaid's "Girl." Interesting Literature, December 2022. https://interestingliterature.com/12/2022/jamaica-kincaid-girl-summary-analysis/.

लड़कियों के लिए है शीश महल, पर नियम इतने पाबन्दी वाले,

फूँक फूँक रखे कदम, कभी डर बुरी नज़र का तो कभी चिंता नीयत वाले,

समाज के नियम निराले, लड़की है पराया धन, बोल बोल करें हिसाब नफा नुक्सान,

लड़का लड़की में करे अंतर नाही सिर्फ रूप बल्कि विद्या संस्कार और आज़ादी भी असमान

Delicate glass castles for girls, step in with care for brittle they stand,

Rules let us not live openly but confined, worrying about gaze and intentions,

the rules of society uniquely differ for a boy and a girl, gender biased,

existence, education, culture, and freedom; for a girl, she is always made to stand second!

In the crucible of my own experiences, the bitter taste of adversity flavored my formative years. My childhood memories never erased how most of society was patriarchal opinionated, and a negligible percentage was progressive-minded, with very few men equally sharing the domestic load and parenting responsibilities, which remain a never-fading impression on me.

Despite modernization and slogans of freedom, a woman is prone to encounter vulnerabilities, discourteous comments, societal prejudices of domesticity, obedience, and emotional abuse, with indelible blemishes of agony. This stiffening rapid rise witnessed in the conservative, orthodox pressure challenges the very essence of womankind. The world legitimizes no appreciation and respect in dealing with emotional and physical problems concerning the complexity of womanhood. The very fabric of homes is ruined in the name of obligingness, modesty, mistrust, pressure on childbearing (preferentially male children), restrictions, and objectification. With peace and well-being jeopardized, women undergo psychological trauma and stings of marital discord. Unwarranted attacks on self-respect and misunderstandings of candid talk as leaving undesirable ambiguity result in her self-consciousness. Women live in fear of social constructions hidden in unwritten rules of societal acceptability, blamed for finding answers, yet in the guise of care and compatibility with unspoken attempts, such painful encounters are either ignored or endured.

The dire need to empathize with fellow counterparts, paving the way for sharing chores and responsibilities with a non-stereotypic approach to welcoming a gender-equal society, is overlooked.

A woman is a feminine strength embodied in herself. Although circumstances may frighten her momentarily, she projects her real strength at times of adversity. Underlined with qualities depicted in the goddess Durga in the scriptures, every woman is a graceful epitome of love, sacrifice, determination, piety, power, prudence, kindness, dignity, empathy, compassion, punishment, and revenge, as the need be[3]. She zealously actuates her inner strength and is empowered with marvelous rewards by overcoming obstacles with amplified power, safeguarding self-respect, and healing frightened hearts. All she needs is an understanding of the sadness in her heart and a bit of encouragement, esteem, and appreciation.

In contrast with stereotypic societal sovereignty, I am glad to see some of my friends and people around me who got married in the early and 1990's blessed with the best of life, enjoying their parents' home and in-laws'.

Michelle Obama, "There is no limit to what we, as women, can accomplish."

---

3   Bajoria, Kartik. What Our Girls Can Learn from Maa Durga. The Times of India, October 2019 ,3. https://timesofindia.indiatimes.com/life-style/parenting/moments/what-our-girls-child-can-learn-from-maa-durga/articleshow/71421199.cms.

3.2 NIKAAH, SHAREEK-E-HAYAAT AND MORE–SOME UNFADING MEMORIES AND LESSONS

Thoughts of marriage didn't cross my mind then, but destiny held plans far grander than mine. Fate toured me through peaceful meadows and challenging terrains.

"And one of His signs is that He created for you spouses from among yourselves so that you may find comfort in them. And He has placed between you compassion and mercy. Surely in this are signs for people who reflect."[4] *(Quran, 30:21)*

The blessings and dua of my elders knocked at my door in my late teens in the form of an arranged marriage, Nikaah-Wedlock ceremonies, and the solemnization of sacred marriage play an integral part in the social fabric of our culture. A new bond between two people and a social affiliation brings families together. Predominantly moving from my parent's home to a new home with my Shareek E Hayaat (Husband), as a young girl, my heart encountered numerous emotions of hopes, aspirations, and commitments, with a bit of unsettledness.

एक ऐसा मीठा बंधन है शादी ब्याह जिसे सजाये दो जन,

पूरी शफ़खत और लगन से, प्यार और यकीन की बुनियाद पे टिका है यह बंधन,

त्याग भी स्नेह भी, ख़ुशी और तकलीफ में साथ निभाने वाले वचन हैं जहाँ

इज़्ज़त भी खैरंदेशी भी और है कई कही और अनकही कस्मे भी यहाँ

---

4   The Holy Quran: Surah Ar-Rum 30:21. Accessed April 2025 ,8. https://quran.com/en/ar-rum/21.

Wedlock, a sweet everlasting bond the two beautiful souls adore and cherish

Built on the solid foundation of love and trust, with sincerity and dedication,

Love and sacrifice are the hallmarks, promises to stay together in happiness and sorrow

Respect and kindness coupled with understanding on matters said and unsaid in a row!

Every girl is blessed with a beautiful and comfortable parent's home, and those blessed with amicable in-laws' place are also more fortunate.

My first step into my in-laws' house was slightly neophobic yet full of optimism for kaleidoscopic memories to cherish. An old-fashioned home housing a spacious verandah, surrounded by lush greenery with flowering plants, was a treat to a nature lover in me. An iconic Jamoon (Black plum) tree open for neighbors to pick fruits fascinated me, symbolizing sharing, and a buzz of close-knit relatives in the neighborhood added to my enthusiasm, signifying connectedness.

My mother-in-law welcomed me into the family, and right from day one, I was at ease spending time cordially with all family members. Her progressive-mindedness, effervescent smile, and composed behavior reflect her struggles in life. The fond remembrance of my father-in-law's care and kindness would spark her eyes with immense love and an unspoken emptiness after him.

जोड़ियां तो ऊपरवाला बनाये, निकाह करे अपनाइयत का रिश्ता खायम

संजोये सारे रिश्ते नाते प्यार दुलार से, नदिया सा बहाव मद्धम

झील सी ठंडक, उगते सूरज जैसी ताज़गी हो पैगाम

घर हो रोशन सुकून, ज़िन्दगी बने खुशगवार और आसान हरदम

ज़िद वाला न हो मामिला बल्कि सब्र से हो वचन निभाने

बंधन ऐसे परिवारों को जोड़े, एक ऐसी डोर में पुरोये

जिसमे हो कई हीरे जवाहरात अनमोल नगीने जड़े

सजे सारे मौसम की बहार रंग दुलार मौजूद रंगोली वाले

Matches are made in heaven; marriage establishes a relationship with revere and adore

laced with bonds of actuality, filled with colors of spectrum, nurturing at best with care,

cherishing every new relationship like the musical flow of a waterfall super

Entwining hearts and families, like diamonds, pearls, and precious gems stringed together!

Enjoy every moment in the morning mist; keep flowing as a river,

illuminate your home in the shade and peace of the vibrant nature,

Invite the sunshine of pleasantness everywhere

and learn to be forgiving and selfless like nature!

Adhering to Robert Frost's adage, 'Good fences make good neighbors,' contributed to my swift understanding of the house's unsaid norms, and I started nurturing new bonds, garnering moments of memorabilia.

As a modest and shy person entangled in my world of dilemmas and responsibilities over a couple of things, I never, in my wildest imagination, envisioned how my life partner and in-laws would be. The Almighty knew what would be best for me and blessed me with supportive in-laws and a compassionate life partner.

My husband and I started the humble new chapter of life by moving into a two-roomed, rented apartment. However, with my educationist father's persuasion and my husband's reassurance, my educational pursuits continued even after my Nikaah (marriage). While balancing studies (undergraduate level course) and attending classes, as a married woman, transitioning into a nuclear family setup took me a while. It was an early, unthought-of, quite challenging responsibility; the need of the hour demanded safeguarding the given lessons, taking care of household affairs as priorities, and keeping the traditions and culture in line.

However, weekend visits to my in-laws' place and spending time with them always rejoiced and refreshed, facilitating profound connections. Going back home was a tearful affair. At nineteen, I slowly learned to fit into the beautiful role, with glittering newness and many tasks to align with.

खुश क़िस्मत हैं वे लड़कियां जिन्हे मिलते घर माईके जैसे, नहीं कोई फ़िक्र या शिकंज,

हर दिशा प्रीत, लगे हर मसला सुलझता जब हो संग शरीक ए हयात बने सुतून, लाए क्षितिज

Lucky are those girls who find a welcoming in-law's place, like a mother's manor,

The mini or elephantine issue seems solvable with an understanding life partner

While crafting new bonds, my yearning for a happy family life in a decent, well-ventilated abode with an adorned future vision started spreading. Our new house, which included an office area for my husband to practice law, was ready, and on our second wedding anniversary, we joyously moved into it with our five-month-old daughter.

Three months later, my most endearing moments of motherhood got shackled in mourning the loss of my mother. However, the first four years of my marriage were pendulous; on the one hand, I was blessed with our sources of joy, a daughter and a son, and on the other, a series of misfortunes hit us over the next couple of years. My husband remained a tower of strength, healing our anguished hearts, and my parents' side of the family and I sailed through the vicissitudes of life. Indeed, time is the best healer, yet it leaves painful thoughts ever ruminating.

मात्रुता पाए और खोये खुद अपनी माँ, गुम हुए कुछ पल प्रीत अंधेरों में
मेरे भाई बहन भी थे छोटे सिसकते मासूम इतने, होश न संभाले,

टूटा पहाड़ राम का ढूंढ़ते भी किस का सहारा,
बस बनते एक दूसरों का ही सहारा ताक़त व रहम दिली वाला

ग़मज़दा कोई कम तो कोई ज़्यादा, कोई नाराज़ तो कोई था उदासीन
उदासी ऐसी लाचारी बेबसी वाली, बस था एक ही सहारा तू ही हमारा
रब्बुल आलमीन

Motherhood arrived, but the pain of losing my mother mounted,

haunting moments of sobbing in the dark, siblings minor and innocent,

uncontrollably shaken and broken on weeping and sobbing in the grief and distress,

sorrow as heavy as a mountain on tiny shoulders,

Sadness, coupled with helplessness, tired, solitary travelers

on this challenging path! God, the only support with us!

Pleasing the Almighty has been more pivotal for me than pleasing anyone else. My husband and I stand by the same testimony. He ensured to provide the family in adherence to the halal (lawful) way with high integrity. A great blessing lies in solidarity and respect for each other's limitations. He cared for the two children (under five) and the household affairs, facilitating my pursuit of higher education and career-building.

I have many touching memories of his eyes reflecting unpretentious and uncontrived emotions for my achievements since the struggling days of my early career. He finds wisdom through the verses of the Quran that exemplify life lessons. My experiences with him enriched me with observational learning and to be a patient listener, a sound advisor, and an empathizer with solid principles and values.

"It takes courage to grow up and become who you really are." –E.E. Cummings.

Moreover, circumstances powerfully shape a person; framework and vulnerabilities during growing-up years transformed my husband into a self-made and independent person. Driven by immense love and reverence for his parents, he inherited sincerity and hard work from his father, a passion for reading, and a heart for the less privileged from his mother. Even as a teenager, with a meager amount in his pocket, he preferred vegetarian lunch over non-vegetarian, at a mess to leave a tip to the waiter. During his early twenties, a bitter crisis in the form of a road accident changed his perspective entirely; his resolve to be self-sufficient, even at times of difficulty, became more robust.

My husband began his career as a practicing lawyer and attained professional excellence with a roaring practice as a reputed advocate; he appeared for a competitive exam and was eventually appointed as a District and Sessions Judge and later elevated as a Judge to the High Court of the Telangana State. Best known in his circles for simplicity, strong ethics, and quick decision-making, many folks value his advice. He is an iron-willed, hard taskmaster, and work-life balance has been his hallmark.

इन्साफ हो कण कण में, बेक़सूर के लिए दर्द छिपा दिल में

होंसला है बुलंद, न कोई डर न शिकंज, सावधान इतने

खुद एहतियात इतनी बरते रखे कदम फूँक फूँक के,

सह न पाए लापरवाही, हो हैरान इतने,

Pain for the helpless, shrouded in the heart, equipped with justice for the deprived

High in courage, no barriers, and no restrictions to stand just

Keep unpleasantness at bay, his steps hypervigilant,

Lest repercussions of carelessness be resentful and dry!

His compassion and affection for siblings and kin have been immense; he prioritizes them over other things. With an emergency call regarding the health crisis of his sibling, upon her wishes, he traveled 200 kilometers after carrying out official duties to take care of her, feed her meals, and attend to her medical needs. Such instances define the person he is!

कोई बोले अल्फ़ाज़ से तो कोई मुख़्तलिफ अंदाज़ से,

गुफ्तगू के अंदाज़ नर्म, कम से कम अलफ़ाज़ में

न किसी तारीफ के मोहताज न कोई गुज़ारिश या सिफारिश के,

नर्म दिली इतनी के आगे वाले की तकलीफ सुनने पर हुए नम सी आँखें

निपटाए मुआमिलात नर्म मुलायम हाथ से पर काहेली और सुस्ती न सहपाये

जमा पूँजी अनमोल बस नेक दिली और पालन नियम हो निशानी नामदार ऐसे

Some express hollow phrases, some with a quiet, gentle demeanor, and some grand pledges,

his style is different and resonates with emotions

Heedless to echoes of tweets around, soft-spoken and reticent!

Neither the crown nor accolades nor is he entranced with any request!

Handles every matter with a soft hand, and no place for lethargy and laziness,

stands uncompromised for his discipline and principles, this possession is most priceless!

The aptness with quotations and anecdotes from books like Chandamama and Neeti Bodhanalu, which he read as a child, is remarkably adept. The deep insight into mythological stories they read in childhood and the lessons drawn make him well-versed with a relatable story for every occasion with quick relevance.

He has been the anchor in laying a solid foundation for both children. As a mentor, he leads them by example in time management, principles, and values, inspiring them to lead a joyful life with an interest in sports. As the saying goes, 'An apple doesn't fall far from the tree,' I saw the quality of compassion in abundance in both of my children.

As the head of the family, he is seamless in his commitment and holds family members in high esteem. His life motto advocates that there is no shortcut to hard work, which begets success. His upholding of emotional security helped both children make life decisions.

सुख में लगे हर चेहरा अपना, पर दुःख में दिल चाहे एक हाथ जो थामे,

बने तुम्हारी अनकही ताकत हिम्मत वाली,

ज़िन्दगी में आये इतने पल जो बने अलामात सच्चाई, सादगी और फैसले वाले

एक सही फ़ैसला बनाये दुनिया और ग़लत उजाड़े उसे,

मशक्कत से है हासिल सारा जहाँ ज़िन्दगी को खुल के जियें,

हसना हसाना भी एक फन् है, अपनी ख़ुशी सब से बाँट कर जियें,

इसी से रोशन किसी का जहाँ है !

Tears and heartache give agony untold, the cursed trouble wretched,

the descent into darkness, stoic though stand

High stakes of the right decision! The troubled, in care long for a holding hand

A grieving heart longs for untold strength and courage for the injured soul

Live life fully, spread smiles, and work hard to replace the burdens with joy.

Your sturdiness illuminates the entire world for someone!

The judicious generosity he projects, even at moments of loss, pressure, pain, shock, or crisis, has lessons on humanness and kindness. On my losing a valuable gold ornament at home, a sensitive incident of generosity towards domestic helpers exemplifies how he safeguards people's self-respect and emotions over worldly possessions. It is impressive to note how a moment of thoughtfulness saves a lot of unrest and regret.

दुनिया के नियम, निराले सबक भी, और है इंसान बेबस हालात के आगे

सीख भी, दुआ भी, हमदर्दी भी, राम भी आशीर्वाद और प्रवचन भी,

जितने भी हो तूफ़ान टकराते, गिर कर संभलना भी, संभल कर जुड़ना भी,

सारा खेल तो संतुलन का है, हर दिशा रफ़्तार पकडे रखने में है समझदारी!

Man entangled in this life tale, conditional though

rules of the world, unique lessons of blessings enshrouded in prayer!

If you fall in pain, a spectrum of colors, sympathy, sorrow, sermons, raise you with new vigor,

and let your speed moderate but not lose! After all, it is all a balancing act!

Life is about love, affection, transformations, and transitions, including sweet and sour lessons of respect, trust, and living by values. Living according to the Sunnah and following the preachings of the Quran have made our paths easy and contended. At the end of life, what we take with us are not the best moments spent but the chiseled engravings we leave about ourselves.

करे हर मसले का उपाय आसान, ऐसी आसमानी किताब हमारी, हमारे हर सुख दुःख की साथी

और पढ़ने से ना ही मिलता सुकून दिल को, बल्कि नेकी भी

अल्लाह को राज़ी करने वाली कुरआन, हर राह और मंज़िल में हो आसानी

सही गलत फैसलों को सुधारती, तौर तरीक़े जीने के है सिखाती

Verses touch the heart, make every track and destination easy, offer solutions to all issues,

The Quran recitation bestows peace, pleases Allah, and instills confidence through softness!

It rectifies the path for the misled by guiding them to be righteous,

our beacon light and companion in decision-making, and our Confidante in joys and sorrows!

3.3 CHILDREN A BEAUTIFUL ADDITION-ADORATION OF LIFE

The beautiful journey of life glides us through excellent phases, and the greatest blessed gift comes our way in the form of children. A mother feels the characteristic emotional attachment much before a child is born; perceiving it as a rewarding experience, she endures immense physical, mental, and emotional pain. However, the absolute delight of easing all pain starts when the bundle of joy opens its eyes to the new world. The first cry sounds like the sweetest music a mother can ever hear, and a baby's first breath fills her heart with a treasure of happiness; instantly, she tries her best to care for the baby's well-being with warm cuddles.

नन्हे फ़रिश्ते कोमल स्पर्श वाले, हैं अल्लाह की देन,

गर्म, नर्म मुलायम काया, दिल को छूलेने वाली सजाए मासूम सी मुस्कान

छूने से भी लगे डर उसको न दे बैठें तकलीफ, खरोच न लग जाए,

ये नाज़ुक त्वचा, जितना भी देखूं, नैन तो हैं तरसते

आहिस्ता से हर आहट का चमकता एहसास और ख़याल

आज भी हर याद ताज़ी, चाहे हो औलाद, या छोटे भाई बहन

Little angels are the gift of Allah, with an unforgettable feathery soft touch,

the warm, soft, delicate skin, fearful of holding them!

Fear! even the slightest touch can give them scratches and pain,

The more I look, the more my eyes yearn,

Understanding every cooing slowly, and taking care always!

Every memory remains vivid, whether it is of the children or younger siblings!

The Prophet Muhammed PBUH said, "When a boy is born, he brings one light, and when a girl is born, she brings two lights. "Children are a wonderful gift from Almighty Allah to parents. All riches and resources are worthless compared to one's children."[5]

The first gentle touch of the newborn's tiny hands is incredible; no words can describe the feeling of both parents watching the tiny one's daily growth. I dearly cherish the formative years of my two children, which happened miraculously in the blink of an eye. As parents, we start dreaming of their future adorned with all the beautiful colors of rainbows and warm sunshine.

Amidst the joy of daily routine, life shakes you to perpetual darkness with disruptive instances, and as parents, we are put to the test when kids fall sick!

Three months after losing my mom, my ten-month-old daughter was diagnosed with acute pneumonia. With minimal hope for her survival, the doctor recommended we try our luck at a city hospital with advanced facilities. Even after thirty years, every minute detail of the unfortunate hour remains in my mind. With my little one put on saline and oxygen, we headed to the city hospital, which was one hundred and twenty kilometers away, in an ambulance. She was clad in a violet-floral frock, exhausted, pale, and weak in pain, mumbling Mum mum…on and off, with quivering lips, was heart-wrenching. With the doctor's words ringing, we continued the journey, wanting a miracle to happen.

---

5   Eman, Sakina. Posted by Aasha Khosa. "Islam, Daughter Is a Blessing." Awaaz the Voice, February 3 2022. https://www.awazthevoice.in/lifestyle-news/in-islam-daughter-is-a-blessing9443-.html

As Shakespeare says, "When sorrows come, they come not single spies but in battalions." Little did we know that a hurdle with a flat tire awaited fifty kilometers to the destination. Already hard-pressed for time, with the baby on an oxygen mask, we resumed our journey after fixing the tire. Ten minutes before reaching the hospital, the nurse on board informed us that the cylinder's oxygen was nearly empty.

After reaching the hospital, very few doctors were on duty due to Holi, the festival of colors the previous day. My pessimism at that disturbed hour was at its peak, afraid of untoward bad news any moment. After a couple of wailing minutes of waiting, she was moved into the intensive care unit and received instant treatment; a ray of hope emerged. My paternal aunt supported me with all the recitals and prayers at that disturbed hour. Since then, any passing ambulance prompts me to bow my head in prayer for the fastest recovery of the patient inside and urge the Almighty to ease the agony of the family members.

The solidarity we received from well-wishers during this challenging time, their consolation through visits, food arrangements, prayers, and best wishes, provided us with strength and blessings amid vicissitudes. It strengthened my spirituality, endurance, moral sense, and service-mindedness. The thickest woeful moments fade with time, but the services of well-wishers during the darkest turmoil remain inscribed in hearts.

लोगों के कई रूप कई भेस कुछ शख्स खास

खुश क़िस्मत ऐसे जो दूसरों की मुस्कुराहट में तलाशेंअपनी ख़ुशी भरी आस

मददगार गायब से जो आये मुश्किलात में फरिश्तों जैसे,

क़र्ज़ उनका न भूल पाएँ, कुदरत के राज़ जिंदगी के साज़ कितने अनोखे और सुरीले

खुदा इबादत में ही नहीं, लोगों में भी है दिखता ग़ैबी मदद लिए

हर मददगार और खैरखः बेग़ार्ज़ कई क़र्ज़ तुम्हारे

People, at difficult moments, come as auspicious stars and angels!

Humility personified happiness for them lies in the smiles of others

Unforgettable is their favor, heart winners and heroes, kind to help

Divine help flows from directions unknown; the Almighty rests not in places of worship

But in the hearts of people, every helper and well-wisher,

Be blessed and always happy, goes on my heartfelt prayer!

A parent-child relationship reflects a lot of internalizing behaviors. Parenting demands role modeling and mutual understanding. With all lessons, life can be a wild roller coaster ride, with thrilling highs and messy lows, resulting in sporadic pressure at both ends. Children, as keen observers, emulate parents and elders. My countless moments spent with children result in rewarding smiles, which include their mesmerizing smiles, moments of mischief, grimacing faces with nanoscopic changes in expressions, instinctively picking up rhymes in school, cute stubbornness, and handprints in books and on walls.

As a mother, I had to design different workable strategies tailored to their understanding right from the age of two, using a logical and reasonable approach. The truthfulness in their approach to naughty moments includes some de-stressing souvenirs to cherish. The significant and minor falls, with bruises on their knees, elbows, and forehead painful though, remind me of remnant scars of my childhood falls. No matter the child's age, every moment is nostalgic, and many emotions run through. Open-minded constructive talk helps their social growth, while spending quality time discussing life skills builds confidence, making them mentally and emotionally resilient.

"Motherhood: All love begins and ends there." Robert Browning

Unfortunately, children are prone to susceptibilities like procrastination, insecurities, and conflict that produce fragile results with severe consequences. I recall an incident of coercing and intimidating kids in my neighborhood. The kids, including my son, were bullied while playing outside. Such instances make me meticulous, as they leave deeper scars on young minds in the long run. I never wanted my children to lose self-confidence, especially during those formative years, so I addressed the matter without losing time.

As a young learner, my son lost the game while playing chess against his father. Seeing him disheartened motivated me to learn the nuances and play chess with him. It motivated him with an added self-confidence to enjoy the game with a person of equal felicity and hands-on. Winning and losing the game worked as a wonder drug, helping him diligently master the game over time. He gradually learned the ropes to win over his father in chess.

Even today, the innumerable instances of sitting together and reminiscing fun moments with my children result in boisterous laughter with charm. Occasionally, children enjoyed sharing some sporadic cases of cleverly dodging me. Sharing the revelations of those cute moments of mischief is still wrapped up in tidbits of warmheartedness.

A mother's kindness along with a need-based fine-tuning of good conduct, and education about poor dietary choices, risks of excessive entertainment, and matters of peer pressure leaves an everlasting impression on children. However, in the hustle and bustle of life, our behavior sometimes becomes insensitive, leaving a more profound impact on young minds, resulting in broken hearts, cuts, and bruises of psychological depression.

At the age of seven, my son's little mischievous behavior triggered a bout of anger in me. I threatened to send him to a boarding school. He was so upset with my remark that he chose to sit in a nearby stadium without coming home. When I learned this, I understood the sensitivity of the growing mind, and I regretted my words. Proper conversations cushioned with guidance soften the restlessness and keep them in good spirits.

My experiences raising both kids made me adopt two different approaches. My daughter is comparatively sensitive and pampered, while my son needed persuasion and caressing until his teenage years. Every impression has a long-lasting impact on children's minds.

My daughter has been a wonderfully affectionate sibling and a caring, sensible child. When she was fifteen, she saved pocket money and surprised me with a beautiful wristwatch on my birthday. It was a very emotional moment to see her endearment and prudential savings, which she still excels today. My son is a thoughtful brother and a scholarly, disciplined child with unique strengths.

In our rushed lifestyle with employment and other responsibilities, their level of maturity, pragmatism in adaptations, and grit for family and guests never went unnoticed. It is heartening to note that how they were led by hand now comes back efficiently. When I appreciate their thoughtfulness, it is a joy to hear them say, "These are the values that you have given us, some you taught, and some we absorbed seeing both parents."

A series of tumults at different junctures shattered me at later stages, and I found my husband, daughter, and son by my side, taking care of my sensitivities to ensure that I didn't suffer tears. I am fortunate to receive much love and affection from all circles; only the Almighty set it going.

Shukran Ya Rabb, for all the blessings You bestowed in my life.

Allah SWT is the balancer of sunshine and dark shadows. These significant lessons kept adding to my refinement.

दूर कहीं कोई तो है, हमेशा अपना ख़याल रखता है पालनहार

करें सारी ज़रूरतों का इंतेज़ाम, कभी तेज़ बिजली जैसे तो कभी धीरे से धीमी ओस जैसे

इंसानी सीफत है ख्वाहिश रखना, नहीं कोई हर्ज, ख्वाहिशें तो पूरी हो मंज़ूरे खुदा से

खैर हो इनायत तुरंत और नुकसानदायक हो दूर उसकी रज़ा और शुक्र से

ता उम्र हो मुसाफिरी जैसे, हर पल नई मिसाल उम्मीद भरे

करें मुसाफिरीआसान मुसलसल अपना सफ़र अच्छे कर्म वाला

Someone somewhere distant and unseen consistently looks after your needs,

Sometimes, blessings are sent swiftly, like a flash, and some gradually, like morning dew!

Desires and aspirations are endless, and outcomes may not come to fruition despite your efforts,

The good falls your way immediately and keeps away the woeful

Divine power prevents certain occurrences; your mere hope will not bring results

Embrace what fails to happen, and keep progressing; the journey consists of tasks and lessons!

Almighty promised humanity Jannah (paradise) in the hereafter for our righteousness. However, glimpses of paradise rest in our homes, in affection and comfort. The devotion and truthfulness embraced by the inmates promote emotional attachment, healing, and trust building. The more we trust and entrust responsibilities upon children in the growing-up stages, the more sensible and accountable they become in keeping up the spirit of family fiber.

जो दिखता नहीं पर है सब कुछ, हमारा पालनहार

हमें जो नहीं गुमान रखे हिसाब किताब सारे

सात आसमानों का सरताज सब उसके आगे समान

बिना कोई भेद भाव सब को इनायत है वसाइल एक बराबर

है वादा विशाल जन्नत का, ऊँचा तसव्वुर के बाहर, कर्म और नीयत जिसका पैमाना

दुनिया में भी तो हैं इसके निशाँ ख़तरा ख़तरा, तिनका तिनका,

कभी माँ में, बाबा में, तो कभी बच्चों में,

फल, फूल, बगीचे और सारी ख़ुदरत में

Who is all-knowing preserves a treasure far away from the seven skies,

A force invisible but omnipresent, the Sole Protector of all of us!

With a promise of heaven and paradise beyond imagination

our actions and intentions determine traces,

Glimpses of divinity present around seen in mother, father, children,

Gifts of sweetness in fruits, flowers, across the cosmos, nature, and gardens!

Although we never realize how time slips like sand from our fingers, the moments of adoration, innocence, the quest to discover more, competitiveness, and naughty gestures remain my everlasting profound memories with my children.

Gradually, children pass each stage of life and have their dreams to chase and pursue; they venture out for greener pastures for career building and settling down in life; the endearing, affectionate elements of fun and frolic fade away, with remnant warm memories. Soon, it feels like in no time, all this replaces an amusing home from a lullabying nest to an empty nester.

तेरे आँखों की कशिश न्यारी

तेरे हाथ के छूने से ख़ुशी ऐसी जो करे करोड़ों प्यार न्योछावर

तेरी नज़र, तेरा हाथ का थामना, गवाही दें तेरे बुलंद भारोसे की,

बेमतलब प्यार है झलकता साफ़ दिल बच्चों के ज़रिये

ऐ मासूम दुआ है हमारी तू हमेशा आबाद रहे,

आफ़ताब सा हो रोशन चहरा तेरा, चाँदनी सी चमके तकदीर तेरी

O, my sweet little angel, your magical eyes, my blessing to be treasured,

The wonder in your gaze is truly unmatched!

And the bliss of grasping your tiny hand compels me to give up everything for you

In your pure, unconditional hugs and love lies a scripture through,

Oh, my innocent little one, you symbolize tenderness, kindness, and gentleness bright

May your face glow like the sun and your destiny shine as glittering as full moonlight!

The nest becomes empty, but not the heart; it always prays in longing for children's brighter future. I am happy for the life choices they made in their careers and personal lives. My daughter is blessed with a warm-hearted, caring husband and two adorable sons. My son-in-law, with his responsive, agreeable demeanor, is like a son to me, and my grandkids have become the cynosure of my eyes. Spending time with the kids, Aayan and Kiaan, is my best time. My daughter-in-law has come like a blessed, fresh melody of soft breeze for my son and an intelligent, prayerful addition to our family. Her modesty, sociableness, and concern are solicitous. It is a blessing to spend time in my garden with these orchids.

My profound bliss gets amplified in the energetic company of young children from my immediate and extended families. The amusing moments of joy and humor spent with my younger siblings, children, nieces, nephews, and grandkids, both in the past and present, awakened the child in me. Their mannerisms, innocent smiles, and pride in sharing their thoughts are all fascinating to treasure.

Nevertheless, the company of my grandkids is a top-notch source of enjoyment and fulfillment of being incredibly blessed. The soft, feathery touch of tiny hands, delightful hugs, sweet blabbering, the cute way of processing information, a spark of curiosity during book reading sessions, playing games, and the babysitting experience with them are all spellbinding. The most enthralling and hypnotizing part is their confidence in gently holding my fingers, speaking through cute eye contact, and signaling their wishes in countless ways with newness in every gesture.

"Memory is the diary that we all carry about with us." Oscar Wilde

वक़्त ऐसा गुज़रे जैसे हो लगे पर उसके,

मानो बचपन गुज़रे, कल की बात हो जैसे, बरसों बीत गए पलक झपकते

जिस हाथ को पकड़ हम रास्ता दिखाते रहे

आज थामे हमारा हाथ दिखाते नयी दिशा, याद आये पल बीते और आँखों में नमी भरे,

तुम्हारी मासूमियत का सवाल पूछना, हर छोटे बड़े पड़ाव पार कर हर्ष जताना,

नटखट और चुलबुली सी हर अदा, कुछ भूलना और कुछ याद रखना,

रूठना मनाना, लिपट कर हौसला पाना, और मुस्कान बाँटना,

लगे यह सब ख्वाब जैसे! पल नक्श दिल में न भूल ने वाले

It feels like a beautiful dream; years of childhood passed as if it were just yesterday

the tiny hand we held and guided, roles reversed in a new direction today,

your innocence in asking questions, acts of mischief, and forgetfulness

seeking consolation, yearning for encouragement with hugs and pats,

Sharing tiny moments of joy, zeal in crossing every small and significant milestone,

I remember those moments! Today, with moist eyes and a broad smile!

Now that my children have grown up and found their paths, I deeply long for them, even after many years. Nevertheless, the sweet memories of all these years keep me awake, decorating and painting a vivid picture. Their beaming smiles have been the beacons of my quiet strength in solitude. I keep sending love and prayers to them, teary-eyed at the flash of a colorful display of their circuses, accomplishments, and progress. The prizes and souvenirs that they won on securing good grades or participation in sports, put up in the cabinet, remind me of their interests, hard work, and excitement that they brought home. My mind fondly cradles all the memories to fill my heart with pride.

However dear the cynosures of your eyes, the children might be! They are on a voyage to achieve grand ambitions and miles to cover.

All we can do is hold the memories and be transported by the stirring whispers of the past. These whispers refresh our souls by touching the chords of our melancholic aging hearts, which say, "Beautiful days, oh! How I wish to live them once more!"

बेटा याद आये तुम्हारे बचपन के वो दिन

हर पल तुम्हारा साया बने रहना

तुम्हारी मुस्कान और खिलकर हसने से माँ के दिल का झूम उठना

बोल ना आने से पहले हाथ पकड़कर हमें ले जाना और इशारों में ही समझाना

Oh, dear, I yearn for the beautiful days of your childhood,

Much before you learned to speak, took me gently by the hand,

I still cherish your presence! I feel your shadows escort me every moment!

Your smiles and laughter as reasons rejoice my heart to soar high!

अपनी अदा से तुम्हारा समझाना, तुम्हारे तुतलाती बातों की मिठास

तुम्हारे दौड़ कर आकर लिपटने वाला स्पर्श और अंदाज़

बिटिया का समझदार अंदाज़ तो बेटे की चुलबुली अदाएं

तुम्हारा डर कर सहम कर हौसले के लिए उठी पलकों का इशारा

Your unique ways to make me understand your blabbeing art

The sweetness of your stammering words still touches my heart!

My daughter, your sensible style

and the naughty mannerisms of you, my son

Your conjoint mischief! How can I forget the delight?

In fright, your lifting of eyelids and look at me for courage! All concealed in my heart!

बढ़ती उम्र के चलते सहारा बनना, माँ की तकलीफ और थकावट को समझना

हर खिस्म से मदद करना, मेरी छोटी छोटी ख़्वाहिशों का ख़याल करना

ख़ुलूस और प्रेम का एहसास भरा आइना बनना, बच्चे मेरे कब और कैसे बड़े हो गए

मेरी जान मेरे दिल के टुकड़े, मुड़ के देखूं तो दिल भर आये

Time flew without my realizing when you both became my support system,

without my uttering a word, how you understand my worries and fatigue,

Sweet little younger ones, adorable tiny bits of my heart!

My champions, my courage, Mom misses you every moment!

What better way to sum up than these following beautiful lines from an excerpt from 'On Children' by Kahlil Gibran, with a profound message to understand:

They are the sons and daughters of life's longing for itself.

They come through you but not from you,

and though they are with you, they belong not to you.

You may give them your love but not your thoughts,

for they have their thoughts.

You may house their bodies but not their Souls,

for their Souls dwell in the house of tomorrow, which you cannot visit, not even in your dreams.[6]

------

6   Gibran, Kahlil. The Prophet. New York: Alfred A. Knopf, 1923. (For the "On Children," See excerpts from "On Children.")

CHAPTER 4

TRADITIONAL REALIGNMENT

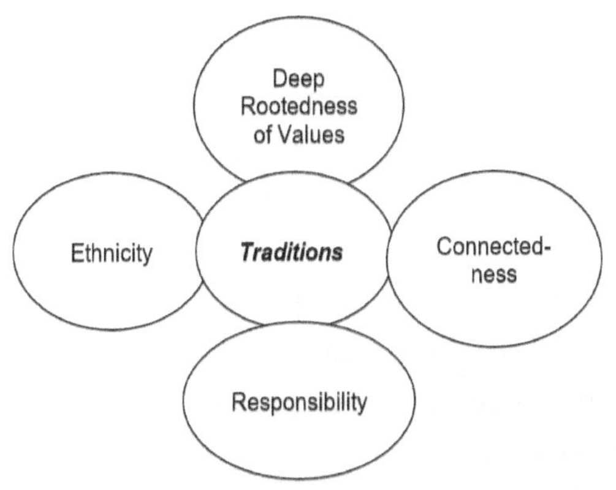

Every family aligns with traditions cherished and carried forward by forebears. These traditions signify one's roots, lineage, and heritage, reflected in adherence to cultural influences. My heart cheers to emphasize that my motherland combines traditions and customs that symbolize harmony. The two famous rivers, the Ganges and the Yamuna amalgamate the cultures, the historical significance of which is called Ganga-Jamuni tehzeeb[7] (culture).

Among the countless blessings brought down as a legacy, the most decadent beauty of the land inevitably lies in the modality of affection showered by people through kind gestures and ways of

---

7 Wikipedia contributors. "Ganga-Jamuni tehzeeb," Wikipedia, The Free Encyclopaedia, https://en.wikipedia.org/w/index.php?title=Ganga-Jamuni_ tehzeeb&oldid=1277680941 "Ganga (Book)." The last modified date is unknown. Accessed March 2025 ,20.

greetings such as salaam, namaskar, handshakes, warm hugs, feet touching of elders, and seeking blessings in reverence with cheerful smiles, exchange of pleasantries, flowers, sharing of food, and much more. Traditions and culture significantly connect us to history and provide everyone with a pertinent sense of identity.

Hyderabad, the city of my living in particular, is known for its unconquerable armor of warmth in welcoming people, with a soft blend of cosmopolitan culture in terms of its heritage and the fusion reflected in music, cuisine, apparel, architecture, and overwhelming geniality in abundance. In this connection, the remnants of the past in written pages or by word of mouth emphasize notable relevance. An array of practices brought down by ancestors become part and parcel of our lives, but on the other hand, we see a significant influence of modernization leading to upgradation in every aspect of life; some of it is reasonable, and part of it takes the new generation away from the roots.

क्या खूब कहा कहने वालेने की 'मेरा भारत है सोने की चिड़िया'

इसमें है अनगिनत रस्म और सौगात छिपे,

है कई दास्ताँ छिपे पेड़, पहाड़, जंगल और मैदान में,

नदिया और झील का बहना और कहना कई दास्ताँ वक़्त के

बदलते मौसम लाएं तीज त्यौहार,

रीत रिवाज़ पहचान जिसकी

हर घर की है परंपरा ख़ास,

जो जोड़े रखे भावनाएं सबकी

How beautifully expressed! 'My motherland, India, is a golden bird!'

Countless vibrant colors are hidden in it, and every river's flow unfolds some exclusive story;

Trees and mountains hold narratives and distinguish every household in its customs,

Unity lies in the uniqueness of diverse identities, making it a signature of our heritage!

हर प्रांत की है पहचान छिपी रहन सहन, खान पान, बोली और पहनावे में
कुछ रीत पारम्परिक वंश से जुड़े, हर घर की हैं किताबें कई राज़ लिए
अपने अपने पकवान के ज़ायके वाली, नहीं लिखित कहीं पर, पूर्वज हैं सौंपे
पीढ़ी दर पीढ़ी यह कीमती धरोहर रीत रिवाज़ वाले अनोखे!

Behavioral patterns, food, speech, and attire stand for the ethnicity of a province!

Every house dons a secret recipe of customs and traditional lineage;

heritage passed down through generations, age by age,

Even culinary delights have their own signature stamped distinct flavors!

However, subject to a lot of learning and unlearning, the transition of traditional conventions led to a moderation of culture and tradition today. The prevalent dissociations jeopardized the identity of conventions. Back then, the houses were tiny, and the limitations were restrictive to little spaces; despite fewer riches and resources, people were large-hearted with boundless warmth and contentment—a positive spirit amongst people at a very young age set aside the fears of abandonment. The most crucial fineness lay in brotherhood bonds, strengthening the relationship, and standing profoundly by one another with marginal divides based on name, caste, and wealth.

मेहमान और मेहमान नवाज़ी न जाने भेद भाव,

नहीं कोई सीमा, अमीर गरीब, जात पात, या कोई और भिन्नता का प्रभाव

सब समान बेराज़, मेहमान है पैग़ाम खुलूस का, बिना तनाव

जिसके आने से छाए रौनक घर भर स्वीकारे अनेक सुझाव

पुराने दिन बड़े खुलूस और अटूट अपनापन वाले,

मेहमान न था मोहताज कोई पैग़ाम या पत्र वाले,

था मौजूद अपनापन और खुशामदीद माहोल इतना चारों ओर,

बस चले आते जब भी मन हुआ, सारी मिठास लिए ज़ोर शोर

A message of sustenance, a guest whose arrival illuminates the house with an aura joyful

Devoid of discriminating lines or consideration, hospitality heartful,

Pouring in mutual affection, open and unwavering, no obligation on intimation of arrival,

Immense happiness and familiarity to walk in whenever we felt like doing so! Days bygone!

ना थी चिंता वक़्त की या शिकंज किसी के घर होने या ना होने वाली

आज की इस मसरूफ महफिल में मेल झोल हुए मोहताज बंदिशों वाले,

हां बातें तो होती है लंबी पर ऊपरी तोर से, दिलों को न छूने वाली

हरदम है घिरे हम वक़्त की नज़ाकत के तकाज़े में, अजीब सी भूल भुलय्या वाली

No worries about time frames or the availability of inmates for visits!

The busy world today, with new reservations and restrictions for meetups,

The talks are long, yes, but with a superficial, touchy show of love!

Surrounded utterly by the delicacy of time in a strange maze!

With a little digression from the customary traditions, a mention of a conventional practice particular to the summer season, which is now fading, needs attention.

"If the winter comes, can the spring be far behind?" goes the saying. In India, summer comes with many enticements, with things aligned in the name of vacations, wedding seasons, and much more!

A few occasions were reserved for customary visits and family gatherings with a significant charm to spend a much-awaited summer vacation with relatives and grandparents, typically by camping at their homes. It was a tradition followed scrupulously to introduce the children to delightful magical gardens in their grandparents' abode, away from the clamor of routine life. Kids would grow closer to them and enjoy the care and pampering, seeking first-hand information on important family traditions and learning to honor the elders and their word.

The amusing story sessions with grandparents were rich with learning and recreation. The time spent in the laps of nature in a serene countryside, sometimes under the affectionate umbrella of grandparents, was indeed rejuvenating with a sense of soothing calmness that lasted long. The enjoyment during picnics in those days and while playing indoor and outdoor games in groups, the enthusiasm and merrymaking had no bounds; it is much beyond words: only to be experienced, especially for children and grandparents. Some of these experiences today have become passe. Today's definition of vacation unlocks many options and experiences with well-heeled, luxurious treats of all kinds.

गर्मियों की छुट्टियों संग होते नाना नानी, दादा दादी के आंगन और आंचल

पेड़ की ठंडी छाया में, लस्सी भी मिलती निंबू के शरबत भी बंटते पल पल

नर्म मुलायम लिबास भी सिलते, बर्फ के गोले भी ढूढ़ते मन मचल

सुहाना आँचल ओढ़े गर्मियों की शाम, खेलते झूमते भाई बहन आँगन में जैसे खुशनुमा फूल

Memories of summer holidays spent with grandparents in their courtyards,

cool shades of trees, flavorful lemon sherbet, lassi served tastefulness lingers, vivid reminders,

Our searches for ice fruits in the streets, donned in new soft summer clothes

Eyes yearn for summer evening games, carefree fun, and frolics with cousins and family!

अनोखी शान होती, सैर तफ़री पर भी निकलते अपना तोशा बाँधे

बगीचे वाले झूले भी पढ़ते, किस्से कहानियाँ बडों के होते अंदाज़ कुछ लुत्फ़ भरे

नटखट बच्चे भी होते खुश मगन गुम अपने ही अंदाज़ में, ईद त्यौहार भी साथ मनाते

छोटे-छोटे तोहफे और ईदी भी बटोरते, कुछ रुपये दो रुपये जो हम कह पाते हमारे

Set on picnics, trips with food and snacks packed, lost in their world of joyousness,

rest in fabulous gardens and swings, read stories, celebrate festivals, and collect small gifts

cherished as memoirs a rupee or two, which we could say ours, with unique pride,

Happy, playful kids, grinning elders engaged in talks, relishing wide!

पल होते छोटे पलछिन पर छोड़ जाते बड़े अनमोल यादें

खूब होती तारीफ़, और मन मानी, मिलते नये पकवान और नये खेल कूद तमाशे

न थी कोई सीमा मौज मस्ती वाले वाह रे ! क्या दिन पुराने

ना हो भरपाई बस हैं साथ, ना मिटने वाली ढेर सारी यादें

Moments short-lived but leave behind precious imprints,

All new dishes and new games to relish, heaps of praise, and pats,

feats and feasts enjoyed; wow, notable days,

Nothing can compensate; never to be erased those divine memories!

Lamentably, the present scenario is disarranged in many ways, with the world heading towards unhealthy dividing lines, tearing society's rich fiber apart, with selective preferential choices and heterogeneity. The wealthy want to be opulent by all means, with lesser altruism in some instances; such situations of lavish display lead to devastating unreasonableness and an unhealthy divide of societal strata.

It is an accomplished fact that conventions and traditions are deeply rooted in India; celebrating its richness and internalizing it is the need of the hour. Favorably, the cultural richness is hidden and enshrined in customs, art, and food, which further needs to be insulated and carried forward.

Every occasion in connection with rejoicing, observance of relevant practices, rituals, and customs in particular takes me to the analepsis of celebrations, among which are weddings and functions of traditional significance, which used to be a simple affair without any showy pomp of riches or assets. There was a longing to bond, and the guests would amusingly stay for a week to enjoy ceremonies and participate in every ritual related to big or small occasions during the empressment. There used to be 'dholak ke geet' where women folk had their style and charm in playing the dhol (a double-sided Indian drum) and enjoying the songs as story narration involving a positive, fun-filled leg-pulling.

कभी होती है जल्दी काम की तो कभी रफ़्तार, छूने आसमानों वाली ख्वाहिशें,

कहाँ गुम हुए वो दिन, बस रह गई भूली बिसरी यादें!

Always pressure mounted upon, rush to work dreams to chase!

Where lie sunken, those days of tranquility and peace?

Lost are the roads to sit and spend moments of togetherness, with a longing unending!

Impressions linger to recapture some forgotten, hazy memories of a few tidings!

The gatherings were held at freshly painted homes, with decorative lights that made the homes specially illuminated. Sometimes, the hosts would request neighbors and borrow part of their premises to accommodate additional guests and attendees. Moreover, it was a matter of cohesive support; the food, even for fifty to a hundred people, was cooked by selective elders endorsed as good cooks in the families; the recipes were brought down from generation to generation. The number of dishes served was limited, with a homemade touch of nutritional benefits and richness in taste. The food items on the menu were usually: Bagara khana, kaddu ka dacha, alu ka korma, or mutton/ chicken biryani, masala baingan curry as the main course, and dal ka halwa/sewaiyaan/chawal ki kheer/dal ka meetha as dessert, preferably for dinner. The breakfast at such traditional setups included dishes like khichdi, Khatta, Alu kheema, chutney, papad, etc.; these dishes had unique tastes, especially cooked on special occasions; as children, we still cherish those preparatory processes, and our lending hands as little helpers to our elders. It all added to our amusement, fun, and learning.

महमान के आने से आए बहार घर लगे ईद त्याहारों जैसे!

घर की सफ़ाई और सजावट बयान करे बिना अल्फ़ाज़ आपका हर्ष ओ खुलूस!

The arrival of a guest fills home with the fragrance of festive joy,

Cleansing and decorating the house for the occasion speaks of love beyond words!

महमानों का स्वागत होता दिल से ख़ुशी और खुलूस भरा

मेहमान के रूप कई कहीं बसते भगवान, तो कोई रूप फरिश्तों जैसा

The guests were welcomed with an open heart and absolute pleasure

Some are privileged featherless angels, while others stand as embodiments of divinity!

It was a matter of personal satisfaction; serving the food traditionally on the carpet and dastar spread on the floor, and in some cases, the fresh banana leaves were used instead of plates to serve food to guests; the unique taste of those items is still fresh to my palate, all these created memories cherished to date. Most of the close family members would lend a hand in serving the guest; it was full of inner joyousness, warmth, and close affinity, showcasing love and affection, stronger bonds, a sense of commitment, and belonging. I am saddened to see that, with the olden days, the magic, charm, and taste are lost by time, thus making it more nostalgic.

पकवान भी होते खास मिलझुल कर करते तैयारी

मेहमान के हमें छोड़ जाने पर होता दिल छोटा दुआ लिए न्यारी

यह पल ना हो गुमशुदा, बस लिए आजुर्दा चेहरा मन ही मन कहते

रे वक़्त थम जा, संजोते अपने घर और दिल मेहमान जब पधारते

Many hands join joyfully unique dishes prepared and relished together,

Guests add distinct flavors, but sadness and emptiness are left behind with the departure!

The heart whispers a humble small prayer for the guests to stay longer,

Yearning for the time to stand still and more camaraderie moments to savor!

बिना महमान लगे उम्दा से उम्दा ज़ायका बेरंग और महफ़िल फीकी

मेहमान नवाज़ी है आदाब सुन्नत भी, है मौक़ा भी दस्तूर भी

बस क़िस्मत से हो इनायत मेहमान नवाज़ी

मेज़बान हो हर्ष भरा, अदा लिए उल्लास मिठास भरी जो छूले ना ही दिल पर जान भी

Welcoming and serving the guest is a host's true joy, almost seamless!

Richness in Indian culture, gracious hospitality, and age-old traditions,

Sentiment profoundly touches the chords of hearts, soaked in the emptiness

Seeing off the guest becomes painful; even the best things turn colorless and tasteless!

A makeover in a few traditions and styles has been witnessed today. With a touch of enormous modern luxury lifestyles, the tiny, cozy homes have become colossal luxury villas with the best comforts and distanced isolation in the name of privacy. Neither guests have time to visit relatives, nor do hosts have ample time for guests. Due to busy schedules and prior work commitments, accommodations have taken a back seat several times even in huge, enormous villas. The passage of time has brought rapid changes in people's mindsets much beyond emotional boundaries, which at times is proving to be unhealthy.

Furthermore, weddings and other functions have become beautiful, lavish-scale affairs, restricting it to the number game! The guest list has all big names in significant numbers, and the menu includes multi-cuisine. The stage decoration and ambiance turned so dazzling, creating a spellbinding impact and leaving everyone stunned. The then dholak ke geet is substituted by an expensive symphony orchestra or musical nights by superstars. The catering services have overtaken things, adding to the lavish spreads. Food consumption and the proportions in which it is cooked could be more balanced, sometimes leading to extravagance in the name of ceremoniousness, thus leaving less scope for balance between the requirements and ostentatiousness.

The simplicity is taken over by great pomp and swankiness; for some, it's a bequeathed legacy left behind, and unfortunately, for a few, it is just a matter of being part of the race and an attempt to outdo in the game of making the presence felt. In this attempt, the moderation of resources must be addressed, leading to consequential plummets. A show of austerity replaces the simple moments of pleasure in giving and receiving small gifts. Lately, people today tend to seek pleasure and satisfaction in pageantries.

Today's lavish, pompous rituals also adhere to traditions and cultures, but some are very conveniently stretched at length and christened fancily, making them spectacularly embroidered symbols.

हाँ एक और रस्म है ना भूलने वाली निभाई जाती बहुत खूब

मेहमान ना आए खाली हाथ ले आए प्यार दुलार दिल में समाए खूब

हाथ भी है कुशादा लिए रूप भेंट के कई,

फूल ऐसे जो लाए अनोखी मुस्कान और खुशबू न छूटने वाली

मिठाई ऐसी अमृत जैसी जिसकी मिठास मानो चखे पहली दफा

या किताब हो तोहफ़ा जिसको देख देख आये याद मेहमान की उदारता साफ

जिस का हर सबक लगे नायाब, पढ़ने से हो ज्ञान में इज़ाफ़ा !

किसी की भेंट लिबास, तबर्रुक या जा-नमाज़, तो कभी तोगरा नक्श कलाम अल्लाह का,

A heart-touching ritual wrapped up as love and affection gifts enveloped in many forms,

flowers redecorate unique smiles with a fragrance that never fades,

a box of sweets with nectar-like sweetness,

a book, a glimpse of intellect and radiance rich in thoughtfulness.

a gifted prayer rug or embossed prayer in holy verses,

spiritual touch, a reminder of true generosity and kindliness!

clenching tight the ties to count on, every page is a unique read,

Enliven the presence of the featherless angels, the guests!

सब हैं ख़ास यादें समेटे पल वो बीते

हँसी के फ़व्वारे दिल छूने वाले

कुछ अंदाज़ ऐसा ना ही छुए दिल, छोड़े छाप रुहानी, तोहफे प्यार भरे

भारी इन कन्धों पर, सादगी वाली ख़ुशी अभी गुम सी गयी कहीं जैसे

The finest reminders echoed amidst the garnered memories,

Soaked in fountains of laughter and comforting caress,

Not only do they touch the heart, but they embroider the souls,

Some gifts seem heavily laced on our shoulders as we seek the bliss of forgotten days!

On the technological front, we are reaching unimaginable heights of AI; on the other hand, the fundamental traditions and conventions to be followed in the real world are being lost. It is our responsibility to keep up with and cherish conventions, which need to be passed on as traditions to the next generations and preserved in the essence of absolute spirit, lest things should fade away and become a matter of the distant past.

The family setup we grew up in taught us a lot; learning happens through observing our elders. These can be matters of upbringing or upholding customs, rituals, traditions, cuisine, cooking style, recipes, and nuances related to adherence to conduct and values. These are passed on to descendants; it is mandatory to learn all these to carry forward your heritage.

Every house and family is unique in its sense of style, warmth, affection, and comfort level towards welcoming and receiving guests at home. We cannot deny the richness of traditions, and the food served also has a distinctive touch, as every house has its fondness and admiration for the guests, which becomes evident in several ways. The food especially has a different flavor from house to house; when a girl gets married and moves to an in-laws' house, she perceives subtle changes and gets accustomed to those; there is a makeshift blend of ethnicity, which becomes a hallmark over time.

पकवान के क्या कहने ना ही इसमें मिलते हैं मिघदार मसाले और घी, चावल

ख़ूब होते हैं मिश्रण ढेर सारे, प्यार दुलार भी हो शामिल!

भारी मात्रा में है घुले इनकी मिघदार जो बनाये पकवान लज़ीज़ लाजवाब

घर घर छाप छोड़े भिन्न ज़ायका सौंदा भीनी खुशबू लिए बेमिसाल खूब

कीमती तोहफ़े अनमोल सौग़ात पीड़ी दर पीड़ी शानदार

मिल बैठ कर खाने में बहुत उभर आए इस का ज़ायका लज़्ज़तदार

Recipes and serving styles passed down through generations are remarkable heirlooms,

priceless gifts that hold a unique bond of joy in feasting together,

The traditional style adds deliciousness to food! Every home houses savouriness in dishes

tossed with love and affection as flavor enhancers! dashed with a mixture of sweetness,

and the aromatic magic distinctly melted in spices, ghee, and rice!

Fervor in presentation, not to be missed, seasoned with a lasting sense, an aftertaste!

Every home has an exceptional touch of customary culinary skills and specializes in an accredited style of cooking, which gives a distinct taste to dishes and the medium of serving guests. Any dish, part of a cuisine, gets its zing and subtle patented flavors with an ensured cooking procedure and preparation time in addition to the ingredients. The mixture and portions of condiments, the marinating, chopping style, cooking method, fresh herbs at appointed measures and slots, and ingredients added in proper proportions, preferably homemade portions of spices, make it patented.

These factors add texture to a meal and help it retain its patent deliciousness. On the other hand, every house has a unique style of plating and presentation that makes the table set visually appealing and pleasing to the palate. Of course, the ambiance, along with the warmth and wholeheartedness of the host, adds to everything, making it notably preeminent.

Wholeheartedness adds effervescence to food while cooking or serving it. It is an endearing trait in every Indian home, especially when welcoming guests and serving them food. A Hindi saying, "Atithi Devo Bhava," means a guest is like a god. The Bible and the Quran emphasize treating guests with utmost love and care; it has excellent fazilat (outstanding excellence) and can wipe away one's worries, welcoming barakaat. Many such nuances and specific tips are brought down the ladder, adding to the phenomenal uniqueness of food and reception.

These hospitality elements must be amalgamated within the boundaries with a swash of the latest configurations to carry the traditional ethnicity forward and preserve it for future generations. Journaling down the recipes and some rituals can be an excellent choice to garner and embalm the inherited culture, customs, and traditions; this keeps the secret sauce intact and provides worthwhile insight into the mechanism reasonably well. After all, these traditions are our roots and must be sanctified and guarded for the posterity to resonate and celebrate identity and uniqueness with pride. Let's keep our family traditions and customs organically intact and enriched by a judicious transmission in a true spirit.

रोशन हो हर दिल चकाचौंद नेकी लिए राहत और बरकतों वाली

हर हरकत पे हो क़ुर्बान हज़ारों बंदगी दोस्ती और रिश्तेदारी वाली

सूनी पड़ जाए गलियाँ जबतक ना सुने प्यारे से मेहमान और बच्चों की खिलकारी

है तकाज़ा तो सिर्फ वक़्त का, वरना है सब मुमकिन, हर बारी!

May kindness be reciprocated with relief and blessings!

Precious moments of togetherness are a treasure strengthened by friendly bonds,

Desolation surrounds you until you hear the cheers of children and guests

Time is the biggest robber imposing limitations; otherwise, everything is possible!

मेहमान लाए कुशादगी रिज़्क, शफक़त, रूहानियत, रहमत भी,

खुलूसियत ख़ुशनुमायी अल्फ़ाज़ वाली, प्यार दुलार वाली

एक और रस्म अनोखी ना जाए महमान खाली हाथ, ना हो ज़ेवर या भेंट कोई

सिर्फ चेहरों पर सजी मुस्कान करे अंदाज़े बयाँ, मन मोहने वाली

God's merciful symbols of prosperity and sustenance flow with guests!

Traces of spirituality are mirrored in service-mindedness and generous hospitality;

A unique charm lies in a ritual: no guest should leave empty-handed,

Captivating impressions wrapped as adorned smiles surpass any gifts or jewels!

FRIENDS-REJOICING BONDS OF FRIENDSHIP

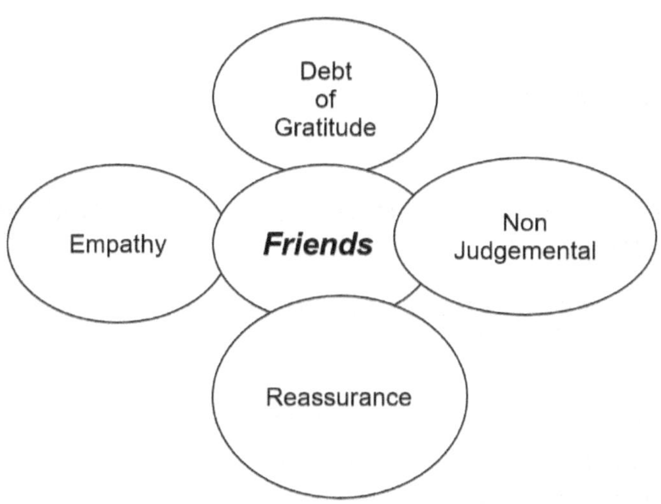

Friendship is the hardest thing in the world to explain. It's not something you learn in school. But if you haven't learned the meaning of friendship, you haven't learned anything." — Muhammad Ali.

Family and friends constitute beautiful blessings. As my first best friend, my mom's convincing style of communicating the needful power-packed admonitions on limits of social acceptability and lessons on discipline was impactful. The reflections of talks while sharing plenty of cobwebby moments in the mother-daughter bond, chiseled at an early stage, had a soothing cosmic influence with a crowning point today.

दिल को ठंडक देने वाली धीमी सी मुस्कान माँ,

हल्की धूप सी गर्माहट वाला प्यार धैर्य भरे हाँ

और ओस सा नर्म मुलायम मखमली आँचल,

गुलाब की पंखुड़ी समान मुलायम कोमल सा स्पर्श माँ

Endearment, as warm as sunshine, stem-winding,

a gentle, faint smile, the coolant of my heart

Her dew-like, velvety, sheltered lap and protection gifted with a feathery touch

soft pat reminiscent of rose petals, my first friend Dear Mom!

As I started going to school, my heart longed for Fidus Achates. Some fond memories with friends since Kindergarten, laced with the pampered and chaperoned visits to each other's homes and joyful times together, are still undried. However, numerous friends joined the list; some stayed forever, and some went away over time. Our convent school symbolized simplicity, unleashing the restricted essence of fun and frolic, and educated us to lead a simple, disciplined life by being upright and hardworking. Neither time nor distance ever diminishes friendship; imprints remain fresh, reconnecting souvenirs that revive cheers.

I studied in a co-educational mode of schooling from Kindergarten through the fifth grade and from sixth to tenth standard, followed by an all-girls setup. The two modes helped us nurture the requisite skills with healthy encounters. Reminiscences of my school days include morning rituals of queuing up at the school assembly in discipline with patriotic songs played in the background. School upskilled us with lessons on passion and zeal to overcome hurdles with a sense of justice and oneness.

Some impressive flashbacks of school days' rest in the early morning rush to school, commuting in a rickshaw, and picking up friends on the way. A notable rumination was that while the girls were seated, the driver asked the boys to disembark and push the rickshaw at the upward slopes at specific crossroad points. The drive home point highlights a humble gesture of imparting lessons on wisdom, even outside a school under the aegis of an unlettered driver, a sense of protection and respect towards girls and women.

नहीं धरोहर शिक्षा, सीख, कुछ चुनिंदा लोगों की,

नहीं मोहताज शिक्षा, किसी इमारत या कक्षा की

सबक़ तो ज़िन्दगी देती है कई, रूप बदल बदल,

कोई इसे कहें अनुभव तो कोई ज्ञान वाली मंज़िल

Learning, not a legacy of a fortunate few to be bequeathed,

Nor dependent on a benefice or classroom,

Lessons many contoured in alternative forms,

Some christened it experience, and others refer to it as knowledge

Advancing through each class level was packed with influences from teachers and peers, marking academic excellence, leadership skills, and arts and crafts. Our sharing and eating lunch together demonstrated secularism and fairness without coercion. The momentous birthday song in the class magnified the celebrations. It added to the enthusiasm for the birthday child, who eagerly shared chocolates with classmates and teachers, making it an overriding day. Participating in sports and co-curricular activities helped us with sportsmanship, aggression channeling, and volunteering services. The little wonders of childhood immunity boosters wrapped in simple games such as the four pillars game, five stones game, ludo, and marbles helped us with physical fitness, hand-eye coordination, and cognitive building. Unlike the latest games today's kids play, these activities fostered rich interpersonal communication and recreation.

हर साल जन्म दिन है ख़ुदा की एक नायाब इनायत,

जैसे बनाया गया है एक मक़सद के साथ, आप हो ख़ास शख़्सियत,

अनमोल तोहफे कई मिलेंगे आज दिन है ख़ास सजावट और शुक्र वाला

मिले दिली दुआ भरी सौग़ात, नायाब रहे आप सदा,

Birthday, God's unique gift each year, a milestone of gratitude,

a purpose behind the unique creation reminds and helps us stay grounded,

Short-lived is any priceless gift; heartfelt prayer lasts forever!

Embrace everything with good luck that comes your way relatively each day!

Bygone are those glorious days with butterflies in the stomach while attempting to flee from the teachers' grave glances for not wearing a school belt or a tie, the naughtiest deliberate exchange of smiles, gestures, and leg-pulling spells packed with fun. The insignificant tiffs to reach the dustbin in the corner of the class under the pretext of sharpening pencils, unfriendly exchanges of tantrums, standing up for support for friends, relaxing under the shades of trees, admiring nature during lunch breaks indulging in tittle-tattle, taking care of younger siblings—an undying smile reckons leading to rejuvenation.

मिठास भरे वो ना भूलने वाली यादें

जो समाये सारे बचपन के पल से आज तक की यादें

स्कूल, शिक्षक, दोस्त सारे यादें ताज़ा करने वाले

जो साथ हैं और जो दूर उनकी याद के पलछिन सारे

क्या क्या याद करें हम, मिठास भरे यादगार पल ना भूलने वाले

ये दोस्त भी ज़ालिम ऐसे हर दिन ढूंढे बहाना सारी यादें ताज़ा कर जोड़े रखने वाले

Indelible imprints: the more you remember, the sweeter!

Memories encapsulated from childhood to the present,

School days, teachers, friends, and adorable bits to reflect on!

Some memories last a lifetime, while some are foregone,

never fading echoes captivating, saintly demonic souls, friends!

Discover excuses every day to tease, refresh, and cherish all the memories

Every academic year began with something entrancing: a new class teacher and a fresh seating plan with an opportunity to make new friends while sitting next to us! Eventually, we ended up being good friends, and consequently, every year, we tasted the pangs of separation, demonstrating that attachments are poor comforters.

This practice enabled us to be close friends; that's why today, after so many years, when we meet, it's like meeting our closest buddies.

जून माह हर साल ले आए नई उमंग और तरंग, सपनों भरी शुरुवात

कुछ कर गुज़रने की चाह, चहरे नए, नई उत्तेज जैसे वसंत

पल कुछ है जुदाई के तो कुछ है ताज़गी के, न है कोई भेदभाव,

यतन से जतन जोड़े हर याद सुनहरी संजोये अटूट बंधन बिना भेद भाव

Fresh waves of dreams and enthusiasm escort the month of June each year!

Yearnings and hopes, renewed excitement, scholastic new beginning

Some dissociation with inclusions of freshness, without prejudice

We cherish each golden memory, the unbreakable bond of best-clasping hands!

Our school learning concepts included fun-filled movies, documentary-watching sessions, and activities like essay writing, debate, quizzes, and music competitions. The celebration of national festivals, sports day, and my favorite exchange of gifts on pre-Christmas Eve remain the most sought-after events as the harbingers of forbearance for oneness among students. The class had the majority of day scholars and some hostellers who missed their homes. The affection and encouragement in patting the shoulder, beauty in the infectious smiles, and turning serious topics into humorous outbursts of laughter remain favored blessings of light to count on at any darkest hour. These sweetest childhood bonds are embalmed with unconfined remedies against the burdens of stress and seclusion.

बाँटने में, है हर ख़ुशी मुंतज़िर, दुनिया, ज़िन्दगी और बंदगी हो रोशन

दोस्त अज़मत है, लेना थोड़ा कम, देना बोहोत ख़ूब जाने

कई हैं साथ, कभी कोई आगे तो कोई पीछे, कोई है याद तसव्वुर जैसे,

तो कोई हक़ीक़त, ख़ुद से पहले करे परवाह आपकी ख़ैरखाह ऐसे

कायनात जैसी सीफत, कभी करें उदासी के बादल ओझल

तो कभी लाये ओस सी ठंडक, कमियों को सवारें मख़मली मुलायम अंदाज़ इनके कोमल!

Joyousness disguised as a giver, grace embraced in life, all as blessings

Friends are exceptional; they entertain and rule indispensability through magical feats

The fountains of laughter light up every day, model every moment pleasant,

the lingering memories in the mind's eye shine dazzling and incandescent

Friends are omnipresent; footprints of their care step in before them,

Imperfections bleached with a velvety soft splash of artistry and charm

It is in nature that the hurricane of sadness disappears into the dew as coolness,

seeds of thickest camaraderie of brightness perennial, they remain the chiseled gifts!

The annual school picnics, held close to nature, were recreational. They taught us the magic of cooperation with enhanced leadership and teamwork, heralding the finest aspects of sharing and care at their best and paving the way to an armistice, if there was one. The close interactions with friends and teachers helped build rapport and overcome inhibitions.

During a few tussled teenage days laden with family obligations, it was beautiful to be favored by understanding and unasked-for support from friends. We enjoyed the little joys of absolute pleasure cum relaxation in bonding together, discussing films and music, and hanging out with packed lunches to climb hills in the town. One person's fall or failure concerns the clique; as true friends, we stood by one another at any bad-tempered onset. On the entertainment front, in the early 1980s, it was a luxury to enjoy watching two movies a week on national television, one on Saturdays and another on Sundays, and some famous shows like Show Theme, The Lucy Show, Spiderman, and some mythological programs that were aired. And the long hours of power cuts played hide and seek as a spoilsport. Additionally, in the late 1980s and early 1990s, the era of Video Cassette Players emerged. We could watch movies at home with friends instead of visiting movie theaters.

Weekends spent at friends' houses, cooking a variety of dishes with guidance from elders, are sentimental memories to dote on. Besides, understanding each other's code language, jesting, sulking, nagging, and demanding rights exercised as cheery moments with close friends were excellent comforters. The crucial stages of teenage and adulthood were loaded with elders' counseling against uncalled-for circumstances and character building. The best childhood days never come back, but talking to friends can be therapeutic, reviving cheerful memories and smiles.

साथ बिताये पल समाये आँखों में,किन को याद करें! दोस्त या फिर पल अनमोल,

नोक झोंक या दिन बचपन, खेल कूद या रास्तों का तै करना साथ में चल चल पैदल

एक दूसरों पर हंसना और हसाना, वह चुलबुली अदाओं से मुस्कुराना,

इशारों इशारों में बातें करना फरमाइशी गीत गुनगुनाना

कभी खुद मज़ाक़ का शिकार बनना तो कभी दूसरों को बनाना

साथ में बिताये हर पल, यादें भूली बिसरि आज लाए ख़ुशी, जिसका ना कोई ठिकाना

Anthemic moments of childhood, fellowship in jumping, bickering,

sharing bursts of laughter in the joy of innocence courteously!

Crossing milestones, clumsy smiles at one another with kittenish gestures,

Friends with unwitting victims of humor or making fun of oneself, others lambast humorously,

The dissonant humming of songs upon request sheepishly rings echos of smiles,

These refreshing childhood memories serve as a symphonious outlet for maladies!

A glimpse of my coterie includes simpatico friends as my best buddies and messiahs. My introverted nature made my friends stand by me like shadows of care en route to my journey. Walking from school/college to home, munching shelled peanuts, savoring the roasted corn cobs on a charcoal fire, and relishing its smoky flavored taste in the company of the girls are fond memories etched forever.

The early morning walks to tuitions, typewriting institute, meeting a school friend in a nearby dispensary, sharing breakfast over the house boundary wall, and dozens of egg trays from a friend's poultry farm add to scores of memories that are often rewarding.

There is no replacement for the bizarre moments of participation in wedding ceremonies, mehendi sessions, insane joy, and long discussions with a heartfelt multitude of love and humorous style of my friends. Even after thirty-five years and odd, a couple of months earlier from this writing, putting worries aside, the house was set on fire, with a changeless temperament with occasional uncontrollable belly laughs and eruptions of cachinnations in the company of simpatico friends. This banter was so hilarious I couldn't stop laughing crazily till my cheeks started aching due to ceaseless laughter. A true friend stands by the test of time, revisiting joy or pain as a blessing by providing magical concoctions of fond memories enriched with teasing, scoffing, peace, and comfort. If some friends are your mirrors with golden lining, some are beacon lights guiding you to a brighter path.

अनमिट मुस्कान और उत्तेज भरी पहचान वाला पैमाना ना जाने भेद भाव या फ़िरक़ा

बस एक ही परिभाषा सारे आलम की, स्नेह और प्रेम का झलकाए प्याला

मुखतलिफ़ ज़ुबान या बोली जाए कठबोली अलग, भाव बने भाषा जज़्बात वाली अनोखी,

नहीं कोई मोहताज कहने सुनने के, बिना कहे समझ आए हर तकलीफ शिकंज और गहरायी!

Limitless happiness, its scale and measure unknown, beyond any doctrine or language,

one fairy universal language shines, a common swig of joy and suffering abridge,

A cup full of friendship overflowing with affection and love understood in depth without words!

Though they may differ in language and slang, they are unique expressions of emotions!

With time, we chose different paths to settle down; all our friends scattered with slighter connectivity. As was the norm, particularly in the early 1990s, some got married early, some moved to the state capital city, and some went to foreign countries either for higher education or to fulfill personal and professional commitments.

It is overwhelming to see the deep-rooted values practiced in true spirit among my friends even after forty years. Most of them attained the highest degrees from renowned universities and are well-placed professionally in top positions. They contribute significantly to social progress as advocates, engineers, doctors, scientists, software professionals, corporate leaders, media professionals, teachers, etc.

"Friendship isn't a big thing — it's a million little things." — Paulo Coelho.

Years rolled by, and many sketched memories appear as things of a very recent past; merriment knows no bounds during get-togethers and friends' meet-ups, resulting in a childlike enthusiasm today unfolding the magic.

"When one's problems are unsolvable, and all best efforts are frustrated, listening to other people's problems is life-saving." Suzanne Massi.

My interactions brought me closer to a few acquaintances on a different note, with time, at later stages of life. The initial reach-out was for a simple talk, and we gradually shared our worries. Listening to their stories was a real-time experience; the only thing paramount is just to lend an ear. I am not sure how I started taking up the role of an empathetic listener, and over time, I realized there was so much counseling and healing happening on both sides. Sharing does wonders in pushing anxiety and depression at bay; the bits of unpleasantness started appearing trivial to me in front of what others are going through, resulting in a strong connection with the Unseen and counting the blessings bestowed upon me.

कईयों ने छुए है तराने दिल के कभी साज़ निकले तो कभी दुआ सच्ची

कुछ तराने ऐसे भी अनकहे बस झलकते आंसू बनकर शिकायती

जैसे हो इंतज़ार सच्चे साज़दार की रहनुमायी नज़र नर्म दिली वाली

जो दे हिम्मत अफ़ज़ाई दिल को थपकने वाली गहरा दर्द बाँटने वाली

Some instruments trigger unspoken, unheard, heart-touching tunes!

Friends touch the tunes; some are yearnings, while others are unheard sufferings!

Visible as tears, seemingly waiting for a true musician's guidance to applause,

Deep sharing shows direction by understanding, and relieving the languishing pain!

"Many people will walk in and out of your life, but only true friends leave footprints in your heart." — Eleanor Roosevelt.

In the 1990's, technological connectivity was poor, and having a landline phone was a luxury back then. However, people had stronger emotional bonds; the mode of communication was through letters, and writing and reading letters from friends and siblings was a vehement connection with personal touch. Some still have those letters treasured.

"Surround yourself with only people who are going to lift you higher." —Oprah Winfrey

The unconditional bonds of true friendship flash upon us, reminding us that one can fall back on a friend at any time. Running into a childhood friend while shopping, traveling, or at functions reminds me how old friendship lasts long and fosters optimism.

In 2009, almost twenty-two years after our schooling, a group of school friends devised a fantastic idea for a reunion in my hometown with a revival to celebrate rekindled friendship blooms. It was an arduous task spinning and leaping to track old friends with minimal connectivity through social media, smartphones, and landline phones, contacting over one hundred and twenty classmates after long years of relocation.

However, the unceasing diligent efforts of the organizers made the arduous task see the light of day in the form of a well-planned, heart-touching get-together on a grand scale. In attendance was a band of friends well settled in their streams globally; owing to the group's enormous transfiguration over time, we all needed an introduction to familiarize ourselves. The mesmerizing ambiance left each face beaming with smiles and hearts filled with freshness in spells of laughter, the rippling echoes of which last to date. It was a gifted opportunity for the friends to run our hands over the delicate fabric of friendship and rewind the moments of chuckling laughter and profound memories.

मुद्दतों बाद हुई मुलाक़ात पर, नहीं धुंधलाए भाव चेहरे के,

बस फ़र्क़ इतना था कोई लगे पल भर अनजाने तो कोई जाने पहचाने,

समेटे यादें लिए खासियत ऐसी अपनापन न छोड़े,

न भूलें दिन बचपन के शरारतों वाले जो है सबब मुस्कान वाले,

Unblurred expressions on our faces, unwrinkled even after a long time!

Distinct and seemingly fresh, we wore courteous smiles, holding souvenirs of old times,

stood at a standstill for a few moments, those festive, emotional moments of happiness,

hearts left joyfully decorated with an embellished childlike smile of enthusiasm!

The supporting staff from our school and the teachers who taught us were invited and felicitated. The thoughtful display of school pictures from our kindergarten to tenth class level was a real treat; we all were engrossed with a childlike questing joy to find and identify ourselves and our friends in the pictures; the boundless radiance in everyone turning into kids was eye-catching. The reunion acted as a harbinger of time to pull around once-upon-a-time tiny tots who outgrew to be true believers and champions in their chosen fields and torchbearers under one roof. The compendium of joy we all carried from the occasion laid a foundation for more on going spectacular mini- and mega-events in 2009, 2014 and beyond.

How can friends stay scattered when a group is blessed with humble souls and the Santas who bring friends together with effervescent smiles and cheer?

It is endearing to see that despite their busy schedules, they undertake these missions, excelling at providing entertainment, collecting memories as beautiful pictures, taking care of ambiance, food, discipline, thoroughly managing financial and logistical matters, and much more.

Unlike family, friends are by choice; there lies pleasure in small sacrifices which result in amaranthine smiles. True friends can soothe mental and emotional trauma with a timely Midas touch.

We crossed numerous milestones in life, and to commemorate a special one, our class batch clocking fifty years, a vision spearheaded the potential to create sempiternal ripples of joy, reuniting friends with lasting memories in the year 2022. With enthusiastic planning, meticulous execution, zoom meetings, and convincing implementations, a Two-day jumbo reunion event, Fiftypoorthi (a term coined to mark the completion of fifty years), was celebrated in style on December 26th and 27th, 2022. It was a grand success, exemplifying class coupled with commitment. The mind experienced a magical transformation amidst the wonderfully talented galaxy of friends pushing aside the hedges, resonating with excellent efficacy that any sorrow flutters away.

मज़बूत इरादा और रियाज़ दे एक संगीतकार को सुरों का हुनर और महारत

लगन और मश्क़ हैं राज़ कामयाबी वाले जिस से हो हासिल अज़मत

उभरे हुए बेहतरीन संगीति स्वर करें बयान फ़नकाराना फ़ज़ीलत

कामयाबी से बेशक सच्ची कोशिश ज़्यादा मायने रखती है बशर्त!

Determination drives a musician to perfection in notes,

Talent and dedication lead to eminence and significant contributions,

A well-crafted painting or tuneful musical notes illustrate the finest artistic expressions,

What matters most is a heartful attempt, which is much more than success!

It is conspicuous that behind the glowing faces of the present, hidden debris of the struggling path to current success lies. After all, life is all about a quest from the known to the unknown and from the unknown to the known.

आँखों में लिए सपने बेशुमार, करते उजाले की तलाश ज़ोर शोर

कभी नाउम्मीदी की रुस्वाई तो कभी आशा कामयाबी की चमक भरे!

रूठते भी तो किस से, करते शिकायत तो भी खुद ही से,

रास्ते कठिन ज़रूर इरादे भी तो रहे बुलंद, रंग लाने वाले कामयाबी भरे,

कठिनाई का सामना करने वाले बुलंद मज़बूत इरादे न मानने वाले हार,

काले बादल ही लाये बरसात, अँधेरी रात के बाद ही आए सवेरा नाम शोहरत वाला

Sparkling eyes filled with countless dreams in search of a ray of hope

An immense glow of musing for success in reckoning whipped by hopelessness

and uncertainty in the shadow of sadness, Desolate and complaining,

blaming self for the failures and complications of time

The spring of hope appears, and ups and downs follow a diurnal pattern!

Soon, the radiance dives deep, with whispers, never to give up!

Steadfastness and grit shine the inner strength, taking you up the lofty place

The tickles of raindrops lead you to ripples of hope, leading to fantastic success!

The group rejoiced in well-planned activities, meaningful conversations, pleasantries, and a lavish food spread. It was heartening to see the attendance of one hundred and fifteen friends from home and worldwide despite their busy schedules and personal commitments.

Every attendee took home a bag full of memories with goodies and souvenirs and a yearbook published with information about friends as a handy approach to connect with them in commemoration of celebrating friendship.

शुक्रिया, ए दिल खुश साथियों, पुनर्मिलन समारोह बने, यादों का गुलदस्ता हमारा

हर चमन से आम व ख़ास सभी समेटे भूली बिसरि यादें, हज़ार करें ताज़ा,

हर पल मधुर, हर चेहरा ताज़ा, पचास साल के तो कोई न लगे,

बचपन के साथी मानो कामयाब उजालों की ऊंचाइयां छू गए, इतने सारे साल कैसे बीत गए!

This reunion ceremony, a handsel, a bouquet of chanting memories gifted,

Refreshing, the dormant and the unforgettable scores of fond memories,

Every face twinkling with warmth and freshness,

Childhood friends drowned in the magical success remain ageless!

No one seems to step into quinquagenarian years,

How have these years flown by? Golden years of hard work and success!

This reunion reinforces psychologists' point that "if a friendship lasts seven years, that will last for a lifetime."[8] Similar magic happened; friends reunited and held back tears of happiness, cherishing the ladder of success through the journey of fifty years.

चिराग ही क्या जो रौशनी न जाने, फ़ल ही क्या मिठास न जाने,

फूल ही क्या खुशबू ना बिखेरे, कागज़ ही क्या जो ना सिखाये फलसफे,

दोस्त ही क्या जो हंसी मज़ाख और चुलबुली बचपन की यादें न तराशे,

बिना कहकहे हँसी कैसी, जो न लाये आँसू बचपन की शैतानी हरकतों की न याद दिलाए!

The lamp stands to transform darkness into light, while the ripen fruit for sweetness,

Flowers represent fragrance, philosophical inscriptions evoke memories of life,

Friends carve out fountains of laughter and memories of fun

jocular childhood, reminiscent of small joys and mischiefs bundled with our earthly life!

The beautiful bond of friendship transcends age. I have made the best of friends with older and younger people. I joined a friends' club in my forties, which met monthly to celebrate the spirit of womanhood. We enjoyed discussing traditions, culture, cuisine, storytelling, and poetry sessions. We also enjoyed simple games and puzzles, which added to our rejuvenation.

Undeniably, friends are the wonder drugs and embodiments of earnestness by their sanguine approach. They become protective

---

8   Hina Javeed -Malik. "If a Friendship Lasts Seven Years, That Will Last for a Lifetime." beingguru. Accessed March 2025 ,20. https://www.beingguru.com/ if-a-friendship-lasts-longer-than-7-years-it-will-last-a-lifetime/.

shields even at the funereal hour of faint-heartedness. Shared sad tales and also the exchange of wisdom and joyful experiences magically outline the richness of friendship.

दोस्त, और भाई बहन, न होते तो यह दुनिया क्या होती?

ज़रूर बेरंग और वीरान होती यह ज़िन्दगी

हमें कौन हंसाए और कौन ताज़ा करवाए याद पुरानी?

कौन ले आता चेहरे की खोयी रौनक़, हर्ष हो या उदासी आँख में छुपाये नमी!

कौन देता पहचान नयी एक दूसरों को, कौन सहता मस्ती और शरारत

कौन सुनाता और सुनता, बांटता सुख दुःख बने ढाल हौसला और ताकत,

कौन डांटता, देता दिशा,अपनी सोच को राहत,

कौन करता हमारा हौसला बुलंद फरमान बन कर नज़र तोड़ अटल !

How would this world be if there were no friends and siblings?

Undoubtedly, life would be desolate and colorless!

Who would refresh our memories, haunting and soothing?

Who would bring tears of joy? And wipe away tears of pain!

Who would caress and lift you and give you a new identity,

and who would tolerate your tantrums and wring your ears?

Who Shares and listens to the happy and sorrowful stories, scolds and hides shortcomings?

Who would direct and authorize your frivolous, monstrous thoughts to hilariousness?

CHAPTER 6

ENCOUNTERS IN CAREER AND A FEW MATTERS OF RENDEZVOUS

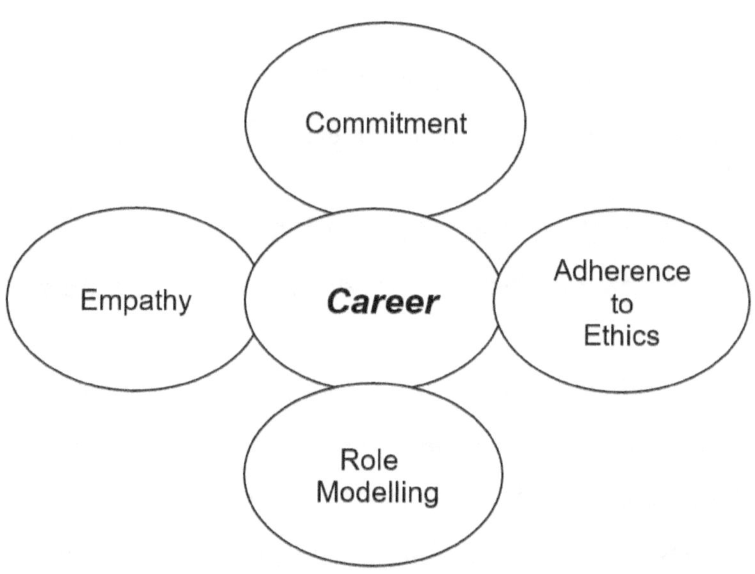

Reflecting on my career journey, it brings back fond memories of my twenty-five-year teaching career. While pursuing a master's degree, I had the opportunity to teach biological sciences to tenth-grade students in a neighborhood school as part of community service. I have always been passionate about teaching; even during my student life, I took up a few teaching assignments. I tutored and guided my siblings, their friends, and cousins in their exam preparations.

After completing my master's course in English Literature in 1996, I was offered a lecturer position at a local educational institute in my hometown. Choosing a teaching profession enabled me to be available to my two kids and family, with the structured hours of work schedule and vacation benefits that teachers can avail.

Securing the job was smooth, and I always worked with dedication, sincerity, and hard work. I enjoyed my career, the students were happy, and the management was pleased. However, the challenge was understanding the prejudiced mindset of a senior faculty member in the department. The biased dynamics of that elderly faculty member in the department were beyond my comprehension. However, I needed a break from the job to pursue certificate and diploma courses related to my field, which would enhance my knowledge and skills for better career objectives, or to take up a government job.

खामोशियों को कमज़ोरी का नाम न दें क्या पता किसी की यही है ताकत अनकही

जो उभरे वक़्त से, छुपे हुए निशानों में, दृढ़ता का सबक कठिन सही

वक़्त से हो ज़ाहिर पहचान जिसकी दुरुस्त लिए पैग़ाम सच्चाई और ईमानदारी,

खुद पर हो भरोसाअटल, हौसला बुलंद शान से, आगे तिनका या चट्टान महारत पहचान अपनी

Weakness is no sign of cowardice; a vital lesson lies in being just!

Tricky though, identity lies in being upright, truthful, and honest,

To live with dignity, stand up with courage and firm faith in self,

Be a master of your destiny, not at anyone's mercy or scoff

However, to my surprise, the unpleasant bias of that faculty member was apparent to the management. After completing the courses and returning, the same management appointed me to substitute for the position of senior faculty member. I realized that vulnerability makes you courageous enough to overcome adversities powerfully, and I learned lessons on resilience, tolerance, fairness, and equality to support junior faculty members and students. When you are honest and dedicated to your work, it needs no endorsement. Your work speaks volumes without intimidation from any corner. That's how my career transitioned towards greener pastures as and when the opportunity arose.

However, despite my wish to pursue a government job, my family commitments and childcare were my top priority due to related job transfers. I chose to pursue my passion by working in private colleges, connecting with young intermediate and engineering students, teaching and motivating them at various levels. It gave me a sense of fulfillment in giving back to society by some means, and I continued my career for over twenty-five years.

ठहरे रहे सब के लिए और मिला हौंसला, एक मज़बूत सतून सा आसरा बने

परिवार के मज़बूती में मिले सीख कई, बच्चों के साथ थे अरमान सारे जुड़े

तुम्हे फलता फूलता देख बीते पल शानदार खुशी से अरमान भरे सारे,

खुशनुमा हर पल, बस यही है पूँजी मेरी दौलत वाली बेशुमार संजोये यादें सुनहरे सुहाने,

Seeking glory through education, familial bonds, and responsibilities to oblige,

understanding children, their needs, and raising them full fleged

Among all blessings, inescapable stand some dizzy spinning moments!

care for the family, tutelage calling of motherhood for children seemed above everything else,

heartbeats and quivers for the young ones, their upbringing and fabulous smiles,

What better to ask for? These lights of life become countless forms of God's blessings!

Over time, I made excellent friends from the teaching fraternity of all age groups. It was a fun-filled experience of erudition from all quarters, including the younger students. Observing the budding, talented young kids and their zeal to take up new challenges in their chosen fields to excel in their pursuits was inspirational. Without realizing it, I started connecting with them as a counselor as and when required.

Throughout my professional journey, my interactions with colleagues and department heads have imparted subtle lessons on inclusiveness, teamwork, organizational skills, perspective learning, and assertiveness. On the other hand, challenging experiences disciplined me on what actions to take and which ones to avoid, making them the most significant, enriching experiences.

साथी ऐसे खुशगवार निर्मल अंदाज़, मूरत मानो नर्मी वाले
दोस्ती के मिठास से भरी टोकरी सजाहुआ गुलदस्ता लिए जैसे

गुल भरपूर रंगीन, शबनमी शाम के रंग सजे हुए सारे

इनायत हो नज़ाकत, पैगाम खूबसूरत शेर दिली वाले

सीखना सिखाना खाना खिलाना, गीत गुनगुनाना,

अंदाज़ जो भरे तेज और उमंग, हो हर नग़मा सुरीला

काम करे अव्वल बखूब, खुशबू बिखेरे दूर दूर ऐसी नायाब धारा

डोर हो अटूट लिए यादें तरो ताज़ा हमेशा!

A basket full of the sweetness of friendship, pleasant and pure,

Friends humility personified, like a beautifully arranged bouquet of colorful flowers,

foliage conditioned vividly, beautiful with grace and delicacy!

Every bloom with a message as a melodious song!

With unique, colorful tunes, bright and enthusiasm-loaded

Learning by humming songs, sharing food and knowledge hand in hand

The blooms and fragrance spread far and wide, strong strings of friendship.

Bonds are unbreakable, memories fresh, filled with fun and kinship!

My career allowed me to interact with young, innovative minds, which was a fantastic experience to connect with students; interactions during lab, counseling sessions, and classrooms were engaging; some needed mentoring and guidance. Listening to them gave me a deeper insight into the young people's vulnerabilities. These interactions helped me address issues with better understanding and problem-solving.

At one of the missionary institutions where I worked, the management made an effort to gather needy orphan girls from remote places, provide boarding facilities in hostels, and support their education. As a person in charge of conducting study hours, seeing them work hard with an indomitable spirit and listening to their pathetic stories made me visualize their plight as an empathetic listener.

Most schools in India focus on reading and writing skills, which fetch good academic scores for students; however, some lack the other two language skills, listening and speaking—the lab sessions which were part of the curriculum aimed at enhancing students' listening and speaking skills.

I encountered some very well-versed students with a flair for writing and speaking eloquently. Conversely, few others were in tears of disappointment due to hesitance during the very first breaking-the-ice sessions. But they picked up the best in carving themselves into better speakers over time. The sessions aimed to assess one's communication skills and ways to improve them with required direction to make the students open up and express themselves on topics and activities planned for the day.

During the lab sessions, a few students sought immediate feedback on areas of improvement and diligently worked on remedial measures to emerge as confident speakers. As moderators, our job was to get the best from them by comforting them and lending an encouraging and motivating hand. As a moderator, I was overwhelmed seeing some hesitant girls and boys, especially from rural places, with good academic scores but shied away from speaking in front of a small group. These lab sessions helped them build confidence in expressing themselves, enabling them to represent themselves better in student body organizations and face job placements in college.

A job taken up without satisfaction has no appeasement in one's earnings. For me, it was more important to do justice with the remuneration I received, considering it was a halaal income (legal earnings as per hadith). It motivated me to discharge my duties to my satisfaction. The lab sessions were a new perspective on how well-versed students can motivate shy students; as each one is blessed with different talents, working in pairs and teams helped them. At the end of the session, instead of intimidation, it was a give-and-take scenario with mutual benefit tapping each other's potential. I would encourage teamwork and repetition techniques, especially for the reluctant students, which made them more enthusiastic about giving their best to their self-satisfaction.

As a counselor, I had an opportunity to talk to students about their academic challenges and, occasionally, their concerns. These interpersonal interactions during the counselor sessions had a deep touch of guardianship. I could get some cues, which directed me towards understanding that the child needs some help and has more to share anxiously, making me all ears to them. They were inconsolable while sharing their problems, and listening to some of them brought me closer to what people go through at a very young age; it mirrored the vulnerabilities of how one can be driven away from the purpose due to indiscipline, peer pressure, addictions, health issues, blind spots, financial burdens, familial pressures, and other disturbances.

With my children staying away, pursuing their master's degrees in the USA, I quickly built connections with these students and enjoyed their achievements and mischief. I could see my children in some of their relevant characteristics of mischief, tantrums, affection, simplicity, style of communication, dressing sense, mannerisms, and many other things that would match theirs. These counseling sessions helped some students deal with the complexities of friendship issues, get better scores, remain focused, and make better life decisions.

Over time, these students would share their results, career plans, some of their hobbies, such as painting and writing poems, and milestones reached in both professional and personal capacities. Hearing from these adorable kids about their career growth and achievements delights me.

जलते दिए की लौ जैसे करे रोशन अँधेरे, सच्ची राह भी दिखाए तजुर्बा बड़ों का

गुमनाम, गुमशुदा हम भी होते अगर यह मौका हमें न मिलता

गुफ्तुगू भी थी, पहचान भी, आरज़ू भी थी, जज़्बा भी था

सुनना और समझाना भी, रुस्वा और शिकायत भी, पर सब कुछ था सीखभरा

As the light expels darkness, lead to a virtuous path the word and the experience of elders

Lack of opportunities can lead to anonymity and distress

While conversations, recognition, desires, and emotions are connected with accreditation

Rough winds teach cruel lessons, so why reproach and complain?

टूटे दिल भी थे, भूले रास्ते भी, बस चाहिए ऐसे में रहनुमा जो दिशा दिखाए

बनके हवा ले चले लहरों को दरिया ए समुन्दर के किनारे

जो आँधी तूफ़ान न बने पर बने एक झोंका ठंडा सा, इल्म की ताक़त वाला

जो सच्चाई से दिखलाए रास्ता दवात और कलम वाला

Not like a storm but a cool breeze, we need a guide with the power of knowledge,

like wind, which directs the waves to the shore of the river and the ocean,

lest humiliations and complaints should leave hearts broken on lost paths,

A duty-bound teacher shows the truthful path of success through literacy with gentleness!

आस थामे, नाम शोहरत मेहनत ही से पाए हम कामयाबी

रातों रात नहीं उगती फसल, उसे तो सींचना होता है दे दे कर पानी,

सुस्त आलसी के क्या कहने बस मशगूल दुनिया में अपनी ही

क्या सुबह क्या शाम बस अंधेरों में गुम नाम तमाम यूँही

Everyone strives for a good reputation; nothing happens overnight,

so aim for a strong hope! Success comes with hard work,

much like the crop harvest follows effort, toil, and watering

loitering lazy person loses direction in darkness,

Be a savior for yourself,

resolve conflicts, unleashing the fire within!

However, I was not a stranger to some naughty and unruly kids in the classroom and counseling sessions; thankfully, ninety-five percent of them mended ways and had good results in academics and discipline, whereas the remaining five percent were in their world of fantasy, with reluctance under the mounting pressure of ornateness, and they needed self-help badly. Wealth, heritage, lineage, knowledge, assets, or any other strength should be a blessing to show you a better path rather than deviating or making you arrogant.

"Teaching kids to count is fine, but teaching them what counts is best." –Bob Talbert.

There were highly talented, versatile solitaires, proficient in technology, orators, voracious readers, painters, calligraphers, poets, and blog writers. Hearing from them is always heartening. Despite scaling great heights, they remain humble and never fail to win hearts with their simplicity and groundedness.

Seeing many students who scaled great heights of professional success with unwavering spirit and determination is inspiring. Numerous stars, each one outshines the other. Among many extraordinary gems, one student stands out with an exceptional disposition; there are warm moments of affection in occasional meets, thoughtfulness reflected in annual goodies, and respect and love in chosen flowers sent on special occasions. There is a sense of childlike indebtedness for the things learned, profound enthusiasm to do small things with care and big stuff with ease, all tied to an often discussed affectionate coded eight point-five grade of appreciation all time.

Every relationship should contain traces of goodness and thorough understanding, including the teacher-student setup, personal space, boundaries of respect, and guidance, with a nonjudgmental approach that goes a long way.

शागिर्द ऐसे दिल से इज़्ज़त और बेहद लेहाज़ रखने वाले

इन बच्चों की चुलबुली हरकत में भी था ज्ञान और हुनर सीख बटोरने वाला

दिल को छूने वाला अंदाज़, किसी का ज़ाहिर तो किसी का छुपा हुआ

याद आये उनकी जुस्तजू निराली, हर लड़का लड़की ख़ास छोड़े छाप गहरा

I feel fortunate to be among students, zealous and respectful,

Sharp and intuitive, a few naughty, with a spark to learn and excel,

The style of some skilled kids touches the heart! Each student dearly keen

And the unique traits on each face remind me of their strong spirit and connection!

As an educator, I am pleased to see my students well-settled in their careers with unparalleled humility and respect for those who taught them. These are the valuable natural pearls that I earned in my life through my career. I say this because the kith and kin love and respect you; the respect, unconditional love, and affection from such quarters are rewarding, making us (teachers) glad.

Teaching as a senior lecturer and Assistant Professor in various colleges and spending time with hundreds of students have been wonderful, fulfilling parts of my life. Being among youngsters has always inspired me. These encounters helped me refine myself and stay in tune with the young generation. A part of my heart misses those fruitful interactions and sparky moments.

अनमोल मोती बिखरे सारे जग में करे नाम रोशन,

ना ही माता पिता, हम उस्ताद भी करें फख्र तराने तरक्की के इन के जब करें हैरान

खूब कामयाबी हो हासिल यह चमकते सितारों को, हर तमन्ना ज़िन्दगी के सफ़र की, हो पूरी इनकी,

रोशन हो सदा आप की दुनिया संग ईमानदारी!

May the scattered precious pearls bring glory to the world,

Parents and teachers take pride in the echoing songs of your progress!

May these shining stars succeed and fulfill all their wishes on this journey

May your world be illuminated with truth and honesty!

CHAPTER 7

PRICELESS GIFTS OF GOD TIME, NATURE & SPIRITUALITY

I credit Time, Nature, and Spirituality as my constant steering agents. They have been my reservoirs of connections and consolations. The fleeting time leaves sweet memories to cherish, adding delight or deep scars with indentations of the past, invariably casting their shadows on the present. We learn lessons and move on to rehabilitate, or the shadow engulfs us in the whirlwind of pressure weighing down beneath the debris. The robust stand against the gales of time, and those who fail to learn lessons remain pitiably feeble. As a healer and predominantly as a teacher, time has allowed me to ripen in continuity at every verge of plagued unrest.

The Universe guides us to significant and inevitable changes through the Creator's stunning design and creation of all entities. The rotation of the Earth, together with the changing seasons, profoundly influences astrological interpretations; everything we consider, including the passage of human life, reveals that nothing remains unchanged in our existence. Dark clouds transform to give us rain, while a tiny seed gives rise to a fruit and a flower; time and circumstances are relative to change; the quicker we understand, the better it is for our progression. Although we treasure sweet memories during challenging times, wisdom lies in thrusting the dark clouds of time and evolving. One cannot lodge forever in the trances of lost glories of the past; on the flip side, one who wipes off the encountered tears of sad memories orchestrating towards the better is a true champion. Consequently, I discovered that the best bet is to live in the present, envision a brighter future, and adorn it to ameliorate the future.

While some memories are fresh, some are short-lived and fade away over time. Traces will be left behind only if people have achieved something remarkable. The pages of history show scores of mighty kingdoms flourishing and withering. Yet, kindness and fruitful contributions to humanity leave a lasting legacy.

वक़्त के घाव गहरे अन्मिट, समय का पहिया धीमे से दर्द तो मिटाए

पर ज़ख्म छोड़े गहरे निशाँ, न हो गुम अतीत के अंधेरों में!

यह निशाँ बनते हैं ताक़त का सबब, करें बुलंद शख़्सियत और इरादा

दौड़ चलो रौशनी की ओर, न छूटे साया हौसलाअफ़ज़ाई वाला

This beautiful life packed with emotions shrouds many charred bonuses of frightful wounds,

The wheel of time eases pain but gradually,

The scars of deep lesions left behind by time are chasmic and indelible surely;

Some leave you tattered and frozen, while others lift your spirits high!

Time is the best gift: it can create, recreate, connect, and reconnect. Nevertheless, the irony of time is that when something is done, it cannot be undone in life! It calls for careful choices. The admirable fabric existing deep down has the magic to pave the way for making your identity through kindness and best endeavors; ultimately, your intent truly matters most!

Nature and its elements are an unparalleled gift for humans in proximity. My silent interactions with Mother Nature have enriched me with abundant benefits in store, rejuvenating me invariably. The beauty of lush green plants, the chromatic flowers, and the enormous array of musical sounds in its entity are rich with unexplainable power to revitalize our senses. In the scenic beauty of nature, in both live experiences and pictures, I feel its soothing effect, with a power that captures the heart and curbs bothersome thoughts with spectacular grace.

During my travels, the ethereal looming variety in the topography of the places, dotted with uniqueness with enthralling beauty and architecture, never goes unnoticed. I enjoy every bit of the vastness and enchantment of nature's picturesque colors, exhibited in the freshness of flowers, the bewilderment in the color of the sky, and the tinted misty mountains. The distinctly blushing prismatic sparkling water bodies appear in broad sunlight as dazzling moonbeams remain captivating with enveloped whispers of beautiful divinity.

Dwelling in nature and its elements has healing effects on our overall health. Picnics, long walks on nature trails, long drives near the meadows, and adventure trips such as hiking boost the immune system with the fresh air and its magical medicinal properties. Therefore, nature is a blessing, offering abundant harmony and calming a stressful mind.

झरना और झील बोले बने रहो सबब ठंडक वाला बिना रुके,

पेड़ पहाड़ चमन बोले देना बेग़ार्ज़ ठंडी सी छाँव भरा सहारा, हौसला चट्टान जैसे

पैग़ाम दवा, दुआ, अमन, शांति और सय्यम भरा कुदरत दे

कवि बुने कविता, गीत गुनगुनाती चिड़िया और मधुमक्खी शहद घोले,

रंग बिरंगे तितली बहार बिखेरे समाये दिल में जैसे नमी ताज़ा

ताज़ा फूल, पौधे वाली! ख़ुशी बिखेरे बहते झरने और दरिया!

Keep going, whispers the lake and waterfall;

shade, shelter, trees, and mountains provide comfort to all!

The moonlit sky, as the fabric of mother's love,

honeydew spreads the unconditional joy of beauty,

Peace in prayers under the azure blue sky is the antidote for all blues

Amidst the music of birds chirping the magical tunes,

poems are penned as though enveloped in the vibrant colors of flowers!

Learn to live like gentleness of the breeze near a waterfall like fluttering butterflies!

It is well-known that nature's beauty and serenity rippled as verses of poetry by many poets left behind indelible milestones and landmarks. This natural gift has been a significant driving force as a deep consoler; it energizes our hearts, providing an unseen balm of refreshment beyond words.

It takes me to my favorite verse from the holy Quran, which questions,

FABI AYYI ALA I RABBIKUMA TUKAZZIBAN -IN ARABIC: فَبِأَيِّ آلَاءِ رَبِّكُمَا تُكَذِّبَانِ [9]

Which of the marvels of the Lord will you deny?

वाह रे ख़ुदाई! जिस जगह पर और जिस रूप में रब ने इसे पेश किया,

यह क़ीमती धरोहर जवाब नहीं तेरे नक़्श का हर ओर सजा!

इस दिलकश नज़ारों का मोल कैसे चुकाएँ, बस तारीफ़ और शुक्र ही करसकते हैं परवरदिगार की

जिस ने दिए कायनात, करिश्मा हर तिनका है कीमती अनमोल!

Mind racing with questions! The wonderful, precious gifts and heritage!

Despite the irony of defiance and selfishness of humankind!

The divine signs come our way often unasked. Does God not respond to prayers?

We are impatient and quick to lose heart; the Almighty often forgives!

Bestowed equally to all, mysterious beauty in the colors of marvelous seasons,

---

9. The Quran: Surah Rahman (55:13). Hafizon. Accessed April 2025 ,8. https://hafizon.com/quran/surah-rahman-benefits-of-recitation.

miracles in priceless elements of nature, matchless stand the gifts of Allah!

Sadly, gripped by advanced lifestyles and modernization bundled with hazardous effects, we must embark on an unkempt new front. Is it not our responsibility to visualize safer environments for future generations by navigating and protecting natural pocket spaces?

With urbanization playing a spoilsport and bandwidth as the culprit, we distance ourselves from nature, locking ourselves indoors in the chaotic four walls of a house, depriving ourselves of social interactions and exposure to markers of well-being. Under the guise of a hectic routine, indoor workouts overlook the captivating beauty of nature, depriving us of fresh air and adding to feelings of anxiety and stress. How do we ignore to underscore that time spent indoors leads to distressed hostility in viewing life, preventing us from understanding Mother Nature comprehensively?

The impressive lessons available in nature, away from the buzz of the cities, incredibly unplug worries and activate our minds and souls. When surrounded by Mother Nature, I have experienced a fantastic healing effect; the magic of restoring mental health, peace, and emotional healing is mysterious.

The next most preeminent thing, another crucial aspect close to my heart that consoles and makes me forgiving by keeping me grounded and strong, is spirituality. These three factors—time, the bounties of nature, and spirituality—are deeply intertwined and have been instrumental for me during times of turbulence. I found answers to several questions that intermittently surfaced in my thoughts. Time taught me the best life lessons, nature offered me solace, while spirituality guided and kept me going through challenging paths.

Spirituality doesn't necessarily equate to religion. It is better to understand spirituality through a wider lens; interpretation differs from person to person. It can be our connection with the unseen, our Creator, the Nourisher, the Protector. It can be a talk with your true inner self, a source, or a simple procedure one follows to connect oneself to the divine Supreme Power. It may manifest as simple meditation, focusing on one point for concentration, something you connect with nature and find oneness with it. It can be a quest to rediscover and reconnect yourself with the help of some unknown power, trust, belief, and faith that is beyond everything. One feels comfortable practicing spirituality, irrespective of others' intervention. Spirituality can also link to the devoutness of an omnipresent dominion that is watchful of our deeds.

प्रार्थना और दुआ नाम कई, जो खुद को बेहतरीन असीम ताकत से जोड़े

खुद एहसास होता है, शिनाख्त और वजूद का अपने

आँखें बंद करने में सुकून, श्रद्धा, और हो एहसास ताकत का रूहानी जोड़ने में हाथ,

घुटनों के बल इबादत में उपचार, सजदे में समर्पण, लगन, और फ़रमान साथ साथ

ध्यान में है बेशुमार ज़हनी सुकून और पोशीदा इलाज

लम्बी गहरी साँस लेने में है अहसास गुफ्तगू वाला खुद अपने आप से,

कायनात में मौजूद नेमतों मे हो सुकून और आराम मिज़ाज

अनगिनत जवाब मौजूद कायनात के दिलकश रंगों में,

आस-पास ज़मीन की तज़ईन नज़ारों की खूबसूरती में हैं मौजूद सबक अनेक!

फ़ीकी लगे हर बहार शानदार, इबादत लाये जश्र ऐ लज़्ज़त ऐसी ज़ोरदार

Prayer connects the self with Supreme power, leading to self-exploration,

It facilitates self-realization and understanding of connection to existence,

calmness experienced in the closing of eyes, reverence, and strength in the folding of hands,

Healing in kneeling, submission, and obedience in sujood, the prostration

Analeptic peace emerges in meditation, the essence of meaningful conversation

with self happens in deep controlled breathing, the serenity of soul!

a multitude of lessons hidden in the colors of nature, the entities that soothe,

countless answers camouflaged around us in the landscape!

While reflecting on my personal experiences, I may highlight a few things that made a difference. As a person practicing a personal faith, I may have to give specific examples at significant points to explain some events.

How did spirituality impact me profoundly?

I recall several moments from my growing-up stages, and one of them begins with the joy of waiting to have great fun and merriment listening to the bedtime stories every night with my grandmother, aunts, or my mom. I grew up in a small town surrounded by hills; summers were hotter, and frequent power cuts during nights added to our plight. It was a regular practice in almost every house to rest under the open sky on the folding beds in the backyards. We never realized when we drifted into deep sleep, amusingly gazing at the stars, feeling the breeze in the open yards. The memories remain vivid from my age of two years, back nearly fifty years from now.

It was an intelligent practice, a deliberate attempt by the women in the family to bring in some aspects related to discipline, conduct, and spirituality in those stories, highlighting the sense of acceptable conduct and goodness, making the kids reward winning and God-fearing. My grandmother and aunts used to hide some fruits and snacks while telling us stories and asking us to do some questions and tasks, and then reward us with treats as if they had fallen from the sky, claiming they were bestowed upon us by the Almighty for our goodness and adherence to discipline. As innocent kids, we felt delighted and fulfilled, waiting for the next day's stories for divine rewards. My maternal aunt once dropped a bunch of grapes at me, stating it was a reward Almighty Allah gave me for my good conduct. To date, those remain the sweetest grapes I have eaten!

कहीं दूर है कोई पालनहार दिए निर्देश

सब जन का रखे ख्याल हमेशा विशेष

ग़ायब से सारी ज़रूरतों का इंतेज़ाम करे आसान

खैर का हो जो करे इनायत फौरन

जो हो नुक्सान दायक रखे हमसे ओझल

ग़ायब का है जान ने वाला पल पल

हज़ारों दुलार से ख़ुदाई ऐसी कहीं दूर,

जो दिखता नहीं पर है सब कुछ देखता दूर दूर

नाम कई पर खुदा तो वही है, सारे जहां का रखवाला

तेरी खूबी में है पेश, कई सजदे और नमन, नमी भरे यह नैन आभार बार बार

The most caring, instantaneous Provider of the best,

keeps away unsafe, bestows a thousand blessed affections

Provider of life, the Unseen, yet aware of everything

far away, but close to heart, many names, our Creator and Nourisher,

With moist eyes and tears welling -up, we count our blessings

We bow to You in reverence!

As a young kid, it was a transformational point at that age. Believing in the miraculous gift, I remained devoted to God, the Creator, and His Raza (contentment, willingness, acceptance, pleasure) stands primary. Spiritual lessons made us strong and fearless as kids and reassured us of God's constant presence with us, watching and safeguarding us. It encouraged us to be God-fearing, truthful, and honest in our conduct and character, making us mindful of our actions and thus staying away from wrongdoings. The innumerable lessons from my elders on mannerisms, etiquettes of life, haya (modesty and reticence), and protection from all kinds of evil were essential in respecting everything and everyone around us. For example, our elders explained the pricelessness of nature and its constituents as the source of our provisions and also taught us to be humble in appreciating Mother Earth. Any arrogance and pride in gait on the earth were unacceptable because, ultimately, the lap of Mother Nature would be our eternal abode as a resting place.

As a result, these teachings steadily instilled the principles of spirituality in me (and my siblings). Since then, it has been a gradual addition and more inclination towards Raza (contentment, pleasing) of Almighty. At the advent of any problem or a challenging situation, the first thing that comes to mind is submission to the Almighty in the form of Salah, recitation of holy verses, prayer in prostration (sujood/sajdah), etc. On many occasions, I bowed down and reached the Almighty for help and forgiveness!

हो ख़याल ख़ुदा का, उसकी रज़ा का हर दफा

रज़ा जो लाए नेमतें और तोहफे बेशुमार, नाफरमानी लाए तकलीफ़,

और छाए उदासी, दुआ या रब हमें अपनी पनाह में रखना,

इज़्ज़त आबरू की हिफाज़त करना गुज़ारिश आप से हर खता माफ़ करना,

God's pleasure brings bounties and gifts,

while carelessness begets sorrows and misfortunes!

Oh God, keep us under Your protection, safeguard our honor and dignity,

Do not subject us to humiliation or indignity in this world or the hereafter,

Dear Almighty! Take care of us through Your forgiveness,

Bestow upon us courage and wisdom!

Since childhood, I have beseeched Almighty with dua at any distressed moment or in case of unrest around me. I also prayed sincerely during testing times and visits to places of pilgrimage. However, I pray shukraana, thanking Allah for fulfilling my earnest wishes and bestowing me with blessed moments of cheer. For me, dua, a prayer for my well-being, is a priceless gift I could receive from anyone. Being in someone's dua is the most blessed thing, and it is what I yearn for!

The moments of distress steered me to draw strength in life's journey. I come across many junctures with substantial add-ons strengthening my belief in the unseen Creator. Many divine signs I received during the moments of crisis nourished me emotionally and empathetically, to discover that strong willpower and determination are requisite to come out triumphant. There were lessons in the people I met. I found messages at times relevant to my disturbing state of mind in the selective writings and the literature, primarily books on spirituality.

The journey I embarked on in 2007 for almost fifty days, in the company of my husband, father, and sister for the pilgrimage to Mecca and Madina on Hajj, deepened my spirituality. It was an extraordinary experience that positively altered my perspective on many aspects of life, with vital lessons on being patient, submissive, adaptive, and polite but firm in following discipline. I have closely seen miracles unfold right in front of me. That's when I further understood the power of spirituality and being spiritual; since then, things I come across have had a profound impact on my mind optimistically, and now I confidently entrust my matters to the Almighty for His intervention for my well-being.

रुहानियत में तेरी इबादत का मज़ा है ख़ास,

मुश्किल से मुश्किल घडी में तुझसा ना कोई सहारा पास,

ताकत बने, दे हिम्मत अटूट, संभाले हमें और उभारे हमारी आन और शान

दिल का नूर भी तू, सुकून भी, तू ही हमारा रब्बुल आलमीन!

Matchless is the festive joy in spirituality and worship

God, the strength, the Provider of unbreakable courage at difficult times!

The Uplifter, the Caretaker, the joy of every heart, and the Bestower of peace

The transformer of dull spring into jubilation, cradle of celebration an earnest prayer remains!

Spirituality offered me consolation, assurance, solutions, and forgiveness. Everyone devises a plan for coping with unforeseen challenges. My life experiences taught me to be robust during challenging times and seek peace and tranquility solutions.

Our hearts and minds are tuned to search for magical remedies that remove obstacles and underlying impediments at a flashing speed, but the truth is that it does not happen as expected. Because God has set up a designated time for the happenings, ease results only at appointed hours. The more we strive to achieve it, the more we get entangled. My underlined life lessons enlightened me to do my job and remain patient for the result; it will happen only when it has to at the destined time.

We are more worried about losses, particularly materialistic ones. We are more interested in keeping track of more advantaged peers and their attempts, and we need to understand that it is a wild goose chase! You are overburdening your soul; the sooner you understand this phenomenon, the better. It is the Supreme Power That has control over things. No matter how much we sob, make a hue and cry over it, it results in nothing. As humans, we are weak at hours of distress and long for some quick consolation, but patience paired with wisdom pays better dividends!

महफिलों में तन्हाई की पुकार का जवाब है रुहानियत

नासाज़ दिल और रूह का इलाज है रुहानियत

सिसकते दिल का साज़ ओ सामान है रुहानियत

नाकाम कमज़ोर कोशिश का ताकतवर मलहम है रुहानियत

परेशानज़दा मायूस दिल की उम्मीद और आस है रुहानियत,

लगे कमज़ोर ज़िन्दगी की डोर और बेचैन दिन रात

हो सूनी राह और वीरान ज़िन्दगी की गलियां हमारी बिन रुहानियत

चुनिंदा दिलकश आदाब वाला नूरानी सफर और उसका आग़ाज़ है
रुहानियत

An answer to the call of loneliness felt in jamborees and assemblies is Spirituality,

The cure for the heart-sickening and broken soul in disparity,

An alluring musical instrument of a sobbing heart is Spirituality!

A powerful soothing balm for the pain, support for weak and unsuccessful efforts,

Hope in the darkness for troubled and disappointed hearts!

It is the thread of life, the hidden hope of those on the forsaken path, the spirituality!

What better than pouring our problems into the Unseen Supreme Power? That was a conscious choice I made! Prayer has been my strength in many troubled times. In the background, the recitation of the Holy text and verses remained my sole comforters in a more profound sense.

Ambition and greed cannot go hand in hand; one must invest hard work, values, and truthfulness with utmost consciousness, lest universal peace should be at risk with shaken tolerance. Spirituality needs to be pressed upon to relieve stress; adherence to sacred dimensions transforms life purposefully. Thus, many burdens are relieved off the shoulders, aiding in making better-disciplined life choices. I experienced a lot in this regard. If imprisoned in earthly bonds, affiliation to material wealth and worldly pleasures becomes a priority. Unfortunately, in such a situation, forgiveness, which is, in fact, a virtue, takes a backseat, and self-worth diminishes, paving the way to exploitation and vengeance.

The soul's transformation happens only when you are detached from worldly wealth and bonds; systematic reformation fades away moments of grief by cleansing the inner self and clearing situational depression, if any. In my case, touchwood it proved remarkably effective; when God rewards you, symbols of sacredness become paranormal, intensifying the sense of hope with clarity. Thus, I confess that spirituality helped me keep at bay interventions and haunting negativities to confidently encounter the lows and highs of my life with maturity and wisdom. The sorry state of affairs to underline is that everyone has a battle to fight, big, small, or intense, whether with your conscience or with others dear or distant to you. We can achieve anything if the inner self is calm and peaceful. I realize that righteousness, self-satisfaction, and a sense of accomplishment are paramount in life.

दिल को छूने वाला, अपनी खामोशियों को सुनने वाला,

दुखों की कश्ती पार लगाने वाला, आँसू की जुबाँ पहचानने वाला,

ग़म के बादल को भीनी सी बारिश की खुशबू में तब्दील करने वाला,

सुनहरी सूरज की किरणों से जगाने वाला, मुलायम ठंडी हवा के झोंकों से राहत देने वाला,

समुन्दर की लहरों सी हर्ष उल्लास और ताज़गी भरने वाला,

है ऐसा सफ़र रुहानियत का दिल को नर्मी और कुशादगी से जगाने वाला,

चलाने वाला आसान तसल्ली वाला रास्ता, आज़ुर्दगी दूर करने वाला,

शिफा देने वाला मेरा परवरदिगार करोड़ों रहमतों वाला

Gentle is the path in the journey of spirituality,

heart-warmingly closest is way to The One Who listens to our silence,

He Who awakens us to the golden sunshine and senses the voice of tears,

The One Who lets us navigate the boat of sorrows in the stormy seas,

Who nourishes a frantic mind and brings melody to the withering, depressed souls!

Who transforms the clouds of sorrowfulness with the fragrance of raindrops?

Who brings joy and refreshment with a soft pat of cool breeze!

identical to the brightened waves of the sea at night, Who whispers magnificence in life!

Every relationship is exceptional in life; every family member is a mirror of yourself by some means; every friend is a unique shadow, and everyone we meet marks every moment special. The resilient support of family and dear friends' amounts to strong blessings we can count on any rainy day. These connections become deeper with prayers of well-being.

Regardless of our professions, we are lifelong learners; teaching and learning happen from one another without any books, but our behavior and conduct leave a deep, indelible impression on others' inner selves. We may meet someone only once in a lifetime; it might be our only first and last meeting, and the impression we leave for others to remember with a smile in those few moments makes a difference. Remember, the time someone spends with you can be healing to others and vice versa!

सांस के थम ने तक चलती ज़िन्दगी, यही सिखाती,

ऋत आए ऋत जाए, ठहर जाना नहीं

बुरे दिन सीख के और अच्छे दिन बने आईना, ले आए मुमकिन खुशहाली

दोनों ही वक़्त चाहे, हो सुख या दुःख, मिले सीख नई

नम आंखो से कहना है हौसला थामे, आखरी सांस तक!

चलो करें आसान हर राह जब तक!

तब तक चलते चलें ज़िन्दगी,

कभी माफ़ी मांग कर तो कभी माफ़ कर कर!

Teachings in the Journey of life, rich in lessons

Fleeting time follows the rhythm of nature and changing seasons,

Move through life unburdened, without stopping, until the final appointed hour and aisle,

in both good and challenging moments, practice forgiveness with a smile,

despairs and woes alternate with excellent and bright times

Good days symbolize fortune and bless us with cherishing memories,

While hard days prepare you for challenges and corrections,

So be wise to emerge as a winner, embracing smiles and challenges!

Surrounded by the marvels of life, I can't help but appreciate how gracefully life's journey progresses. It starts out as a pearl in an oyster, sheltered and handled with care. Then, it folds and unfolds through the natural rhythms and calms down to shine in the beautiful sunrises and mesmerizing sunsets of warm summers. Moreover, life defines us by refining us into a beautiful soul renewed to bloom in the fresh breeze of spring and fosters love and empathy.

Self-satisfaction matters substantially, and our responsibility lies in being reasonable and counting the blessings and favors bestowed upon us before calculating the unfulfilled wishes or missed moments in life. Despite many blessings, we pathetically become prey to numerous unanswered questions. Nature and the cosmos have answers to all those questions. Regrettably, we pay less attention to the answers hidden in the universe. Though there are messages about detachment in the dried fallen leaves, the tender pleasures of winter exemplify newness, waiting to care and wrap the souls with open doors of hope.

Nature teaches us to be like pebbles, which remain unscathed despite being immersed in the troubled foams and lather of streams and rivers and never lose their shine.

Cozy homes, lofty palaces, premier books, and libraries fail to answer some simple life questions. Yet, the answers are evident in the gloomy, quiet, deep eyes of those swaddled in a fragile circle, leading solitary lives in orphanages, shelterless streets, and in the confines of abandonment of destiny. Despite all that enumerating pain of mourning memories, they courageously march in fortitude towards the gates of heaven in the continuity of hope and remain steadfastly resolute to face any adversity.

Ultimately, life is not about what we see; it is a crusade, and one needs to be modest in finding numerous answers in tranquility. The annals of time testify to the solace offered by Nature and Spirituality with bountiful invocations. To carve a niche and establish self-identity, one must unmask deceptiveness and prejudices to have the strength to overcome boundaries, biases, and identity crises with the right intentions and strong values over time.

True strength comes from embracing your authentic self, keeping deception at bay, honoring the flow of time, and aligning with the blessings of Nature. Armed with optimism, let's cherish fortunate days, understand the purpose of life in an extensive domain with a laser focus, and build inner courage to radiate the light of wisdom endlessly.

Today, looking at the fanatic acquisitive world around me, I was struck by a heart-touching sentence said by a learned person during one of my interactions: "People have complaints despite being blessed with health, wealth, a loving family, friends, and fortune, but on the flip side, think of those few who have no one to complain to."

And also, how rightly Oscar Wilde said it!

"True contentment is not having everything, but being satisfied with everything you have."

It is a long journey, and spirituality conceivably empowers us through mindfulness and facilitates healing during challenging emotional crises, allowing us to recover with calmness, cheer, and enduring smiles! From all my life's lessons, spirituality and kindness in Nature became my anchor of contentment. It undeniably rewards me with discipline as a boon that never goes obsolete.

रुहानियत में हो जब इज़ाफ़ा, एहसान, असूल, हद, खैर व हिफाज़त के हो मुआमिलात

ज़ुबान पर न कोइ शिकायत जैसे बंद लिफाफा, संजोने वाली हो बात,

बेइज़्ज़ती, रुस्वाई हो दूर, हो खैर नियति के दारोमदार, हर दिखावट की ढाल से दूर,

सच्चे, समझदार, सतर्क, महफ़ूज़, खुद ऐतेमादि (आत्मविश्वासी) बने रहने से छाए मुमकिन नूर

अच्छी लिखावट और उम्दा सबक ख़ुशी में इज़ाफ़ा हैं करते!

सफ़लता के मंच पर अपना सर ऊंचा रखें

ढेर सारी नेक ख़्वाहिशात, शुभकामनाएं मुन्तज़िर, साथ रहने में है लुत्फ़!

खता माफ़ तमाम, करें बेग़ार्ज़ इबादत, नेक तमन्ना से अता हो नीयत साफ़!

Insights on spirituality enhance favors to cherish and add protection,

Beneficence, purpose, and principles-guard boundaries without complaints!

Away from the shields of insult, little blessings are worth counting and treasure!

Truthfulness, sensibleness, and vigilance keep us away from the shields of hypocrisy!

Lessons in good writing contribute joy, inspire us to hold heads high on the podium of success,

Standing by all is a pleasure! Nobleness in deeds unquestionably is a source of cheers!

Cocooned with the genuine wishes of good luck and happiness!

Intent matters most for success, which lies in reverence and honoring the gift of LIFE!

दुनिया के चमकते साज़ ओ सामान का है ज़ेवर नकली दिखावा!

खुदा तो सिर्फ दिलों को है देखता और नीयत है परखता,

नीयत के मुआमिले जहाँ हो पाक खालिस सब है मुमकिन,

इबादत भी तो होती है दिल ही से, जो हो मिज़ाज और ख्यालों का दर्पन,

झाँक कर किस ने देखा, दिल के भेद औरों से तो छुपा सकते हो,

क्या अपने ज़मीर से, और परवरदिगार से पोशीदा रख पाओगे?

The glare of the world can be a deceptive hideous monster,

Some may uncaringly indulge in worldly matters and justify them right!

God sees the intentions of the hearts rather than appearances,

True worship comes from the hearts;

while one can keep matters encased from others,

Will we be able to mask the truth from our conscience and God?

www.ingramcontent.com/pod-product-compliance
Lightning Source LLC
Chambersburg PA
CBHW031629170726
47990CB00017B/427